IN RELATION
TO MEN

Part 1

By

ELIZABETH HAMILTON

In Relation to Men Part 1
Authored by Elizabeth Hamilton
© Elizabeth Hamilton 2021
Cover Design: Marcia M Publishing House

Edited by Marcia M Publishing House Editorial Team Published by
Marcia M Spence of Marcia M Publishing House, West Bromwich,
West Midlands the UNITED KINGDOM B71 1JB

MARCIA M
PUBLISHING HOUSE

www.marciampublishing.com

Introduction

For many years I had a very dim view of men. I had not had a permanent decent male role model in my life growing up.

I did meet a few males in my childhood, teenage years and beyond, who gave me great hope for the future. Give thanks to Mr Denroy Morgan, Mr Balmore Ellis, Columbus, Mr Esa Guy, Honey Bee, Mr Leeroy Jeoffrey, Mr Lascell Williams, Mr Linford Sweeny, Akiem Mundell and Kemoy Walker to name a few. Because of these men, I believed that things could be so much more, days could get brighter and that not all men are the same.

The Most High has indeed provided the Earth, a species of great variety on a scale from mental weakness to spiritual wealth.

Ultimately, I conducted relationships with males who were no better than those who had created the vile opinions I held on them. Rapists, pimps, cowards and, mainly, liars were who I had met along my road to realisation. I also created memories with men of true spirit, kind hearts and great minds. I am ever grateful for having been in their presence and thank them for the many moments their lights have shone in my life at times when the shadows have seemed dark.

Eventually, I came to the realisation that sometimes, bad things just happen. In acknowledging painful emotions derived from traumatic events, you can work your way past them.

Dreams that you may have forgotten or just left in some age of life to wilt, can actually become your reality. Please note I say working past and not through because I believe life's journey to be a marathon. We will all reach the finish line; however, we will pass and encounter hurdles on the way there. And some of those hurdles may well cause injury. Still, our timing on reaching each checkpoint is dependent on individual speed, balance and stamina, it is what allows those hurdles to become the makings of us.

I held my own person, or being, in such low esteem, unaware of the strength manifesting itself in all my hurt. I mistreated myself; I did not know how to love or be loved in the way my soul needed at that time. I mistreated myself because I was neither taught how to love nor how to relate to the opposite gender. I mistreated myself because I knew no better.

I grew sick of hearing women complain about there no longer being any Princes out there and the jokes about how all the good men, had chosen to be with a good man themselves. This way of thinking could not be right, and if it was, then what was the cause and what is the solution? I didn't want my future children to hear me speaking like that. Those words of despair being cocktailed with nicotine and uncomfortable laughter. They couldn't have really found humour in what they were saying. No woman with warm blood running through her veins would find the conclusion of being left with no good man even slightly humorous.

I always had a dream that one day, when the Most High saw it fitting, my King would come for me. One day I would not even notice the hurdles along my path due to my gliding over them so gracefully and with such ease, hand in hand with my soulmate. I think I dreamt this first when I was very young, maybe five or six years old. During my teenage years, I put that dream to one side as my reality was in full agreement with the complaining women I mentioned previously. I felt that my experience conflicted so detrimentally with the fantasies my heart and subconscious had created, that my only option was to turn into my own personal psychoanalyst investigator.

I would analyse life, my actions, the actions of others and I would figure out why if females were being born and raised with a Princess self-perception, the same was not being done with the opposite sex. At what point in life did the males lose self-respect, so much so, that they would allow their interactions to leave scorch marks on the pathway to the heart of a person they must have admired at some point.

Who were the females or so-called Queens who had raised these males as bastards instead of Princes? Who were the wastemen or self-proclaimed kings who had failed to provide their heirs with a true image of male regality?

Holding steadfast to my belief in a greater power and the non-expiring existence of karma, I travelled my head versus heart convictions journey to a place of focus and determination.

I eventually came to the overstanding that love conquers all. Everything heals with time and time itself, is ever-changing.

A man is just a man, but given the right tools, love and nurturing, any male will have the option to choose to become a King!

I use music and art to assist me during my low moods and times of distress. I have tried to encompass each relationship's emotion within a song to paint the picture my words may or may not deliver.

To my two handsome Princes, may you always know that you have the choice to be nothing less than royalty.

To the Parents who read this, I pray my story gives birth to understanding, strength in honesty and a greater love within your relationships.

To the readers who identify with any part of this book, may you be empowered in whichever way necessary.

The First Male
Chapter One

He who assisted my mother in the natural biological conception of my physical being.

'Honour thy Mother and Father, that thy days might be longer on this earth'... My mother drummed this verse into my mind lest I forget.

I grew knowing my mother as a single parent to four daughters. A wife, for a short time, which seemed so much longer then, than it does now. Always a hard worker (apart from when she was calling for me to come upstairs and pass her the remote, which would usually be sat on the dresser across from the bed she'd be laying in at the time) a woman of faith, just like her mother before her, and an excellent hostess.

I witnessed many times her happiness beaming through like sunshine on a rainy day. I saw many a sad hour, along with a good many heavy-hearted struggles in her attempt to raise us the best way she knew how.

She was more of a disciplinarian than a friend, but I saw her soft side many times. I saw how caring and nurturing she could be but dismayed with the constant battle she fought with herself over the type of parent she felt she should be and the type of parent she wanted to be. I'll tell you more about my experience of her as a daughter inside my book, *'The Women in Me.'*

I did not know my father. Oh, I knew who he was and what he visually looked like, but I could not remember the experience of having him relate to me as a daughter and doing the things other girls spoke about doing with their dads.

I could never relate when the girls at school spoke about the little private talks, they shared unbeknown to their mothers, or the pet names they had for family members. Being read a story by him before bed or being tucked-in the way that only he knew how. This talk was all foreign to me, the stuff that I saw in movies. I had no memories which I could share with my friends, and that saddened me deeply. I felt as if something about me had made me unworthy of being cared for in that way by my dad.

Maybe it was my dark complexion. My father was relatively light-skinned, and I looked nothing like him with my Mocha, dark chocolate complexion. Maybe it was my eczema. It made my skin darker and coarse in patches, and the feel was not smooth like human skin, but bumpy and uneven, more reptile-like. It was really very dry in some parts and sometimes when it flared up, it cracked and wept or bled in the creases. It was unattractive and painful to look at. Even a few doctors had looked at my skin with disgust when they first saw it, and they were medically trained, so who could blame my father, if he so happened to feel the same way. Maybe it was my skinny ankles. My mother used to always say that I had inherited her chicken legs. Maybe it was my voice. It was quite high in pitch, and when I got excited (which was nearly every time my dad showed up), it rose about two octaves higher.

Don't get me wrong, I didn't feel different to the majority of those around me. Those with complexions the same as mine and that of my family. The visiting or absent father was a normality in my culture.

They spoke of nuclear families in school, and my teacher had inaccurately told me that because my parents had separated, that was what mine was. We hadn't been through a nuclear war, so I never understood this term. There was nothing at all regarding chemicals or chemical weaponry that had anything to do with my parents' separation, but my teacher told me that this was the politically correct terminology to be used for our cultural conduct. It seemed to me at the time to be a systematic way of categorising or degrading families who are non-compliant to the structures encouraged by any particular government, but that is for another story.

I did not understand why my father didn't want to get to know me the way I wanted to get to know him. I just wanted him to see that I loved him purely because he was my dad. It didn't matter what anyone else thought of him, and I simply wasn't sure that he knew me well enough to love me back.

I didn't get to know him as an individual, I just knew that he was my dad. He was the man responsible for my being, and for that reason, I had to show him some form of respect. More than any other male I met in life could hope to gain from me, with communication as sparse as ours. This man received an unbiased, unconditional and unrequited kind of love just because he possessed an army of semen that were strong enough to warrior their way beyond the brutal defenders of my mother's vaginal pearls.

He had never picked me up when I had fallen over, and he had never held my hand as we walked through the park. We had never walked through a park. We didn't do any father/daughter activities that I can recall.

We didn't have scheduled visits. It was only on the rare occasion that I would have any forewarning of his arrival. He would come to collect me averagely, once, or twice a year and take me to run around with my brothers in the middle of a shopping centre we knew as The Precinct, not too far from our house, while he spent the little time he had with us, standing in the Bookies socialising with his associates.

Sometimes on our visits there, he would treat us all to food cooked from a house nearby The Precinct. I can remember how we could smell the freshly cooked chicken and dumplings when standing at one of the shopping centres entrances, so any time we were there with dad, and he started to walk in the direction of that house, we knew we were in for a treat.

We all knew the chef, he was a good friend of our father. He and his wife knew my mother also, and they were always kind to me, especially as I was always the only girl amongst three or four boys. I hadn't met that many of my paternal sisters at that point, maybe two or three. I watched how this man and his wife seemed to co-operate so well in raising their children and running this business from their home. They cooked together too and while I enjoyed watching males cook as their movements in the kitchen are so very different to the way females are, i.e., the interactions with fire and water, the speed and manner in which the different foods are handled. The way they both danced around each other in this slim galley-shaped space was almost magical. She served, while he cooked or seasoned the next batch of chicken or goat, in these white plastic containers that I used to think were midway between the size of my wash bucket and a barrel. After visiting a wholesaler, I realised that they were just catering sized containers. My thoughts on them being close to the size of a barrel were an extreme exaggeration but compared to the containers and bowls my mum and my granny used, they seemed huge.

She completed chores with one child, while another would be peeling vegetables. She would wash dishes helping with literature assignments, while he assisted with maths homework. They shared the same vision, and they were both putting their all into supporting each other to get through each day. He used to call his daughter to come and play with me, and in my mind, it seemed like it was sunny days every time we went there.

I imagined one day my husband would dance with me around our kitchen and we'd tag team with our children too. That life flowed with the image of the family life I wanted. I wanted to cook, learn, and laugh with my children, more than I worked away from them. That is still my aim.

Days spent out with my dad felt like so much fun to me then. I longed for and craved his intervention so much in my earlier years.

Sometimes when he came for just me, we would go to my older brother, Edris's home and dad would leave me by myself in the living room. He never seemed to notice the discomfort I felt. I would sit there looking at the many clashing shades, colours and designs of florals, which covered every inch of the room, from the floor to the sofas, from the cushions to the wallpaper and curtains to door panels. Then there were crocheted doilies, and armrests also and they seemed to be in several different designs too. My Grandmother had lots of these crocheted and knitted doilies, though she had themed each room with particular styles. The doilies which had a Flamenco dress style edge always sat beneath a crystal centrepiece, flower vase or fruit bowl. These were very common in those days, but Edris's mum had so much of it.

There was a colourful parrot or talking budgie, which squawked louder than the television when it wanted attention. Its voice was high pitched, piercing, annoying, and it proper freaked me out. It reminded me of one that I had seen in one of the James Bond films my mum had made me watch.

It usually took at least a good six or seven Top Cat cartoons for dad to come back and what I can only describe as him rescuing me from petal palpitations when Edris wasn't home. It felt like an eternity sometimes.

When my brother was there, we'd sit in the kitchen together. He was always eating and would usually make me a smaller version of whatever he made for himself. His mum had bar stools placed at an island breakfast bar which spun around, and I loved the fact that my feet couldn't touch the floor, so Edris had to lift me off and on to them.

I adored the brother whose home it was, and his mother was fine to get along with too, but I so detested the decoration of that room that I dreaded visiting. It later gave me a complex about overpowering floral designs. It created this dark anxiety whenever I'm in a room where more than two different flowery patterns meet.

It disturbs me to this day to find more than one floral print in a room, yet I now love flowered gardens even more than I did then and find a great sense of peace being in them. I acknowledge now that paradise is in one's mind and that room was Edris's mother's way of physically taking herself as close to that image of paradise as she could, while enduring life in the grey, concrete jungle she had left her Caribbean home for. It's crazy how paradigms can shift your perspective on things.

On the odd occasion, my dad would take me to another of his friend's homes. I liked this friend a lot and was ever so grateful when this was my father's destination. She was a slim, classy, chic, pretty lady, like the ones from the TV show, Dynasty. I think she was the first woman I met with a dress sense I truly admired. Whether she was in conservative daywear, comfortable social wear or still in her pyjamas, she looked sleek. Her hair always looked good, and her fingernails were consistently well manicured. She was so nice to me whenever we went there. Before her my father disappeared, she always made sure I had snacks, a drink, and the remote control. She would come to check on me sometimes and give me chocolates in secret.

Funny thing was, I already knew this woman as she was the mother of one of my elder sister's friends. We never spoke of this in front of her daughters and I never spoke of my father's visits to my sister. We had a mutual unspoken, understanding and regardless of who had taken me to her home, she was always extra nice to me whenever I was there. I wonder if she knew I was in awe of her. I used to secretly wish my dad would fall in love and marry her so that she'd be my stepmother. My wish was not granted.

I had always yearned for a brother growing up and my mother had told me that it was because my older brother, Barrington, was living with us when I was a baby. That I had experienced his presence and my subconscious was most likely registering him returning to his mother as a loss. He had lived with us for a couple of years, so this resonated and seemed to fit as a perfectly rational explanation for my yearning. (As the story continues, I found a more justifiable reason for it).

My father had lived with my mother until I was around three years of age, so I don't remember much about what it was like to live in a two-parent home. Barrington and my sisters have shared stories of their past living with him, they had many memories. I revelled in hearing them.

I sometimes imagined myself being at the scene watching from close by but wearing an invisibility cape (like Sheila), so as not to disturb the setting. There were shopping trips to The Precinct, days out visiting family friends and what sounded like lots of fun times between my siblings. There were also some awfully distressing disciplinary sessions, for which, I was grateful not to remember.

Present thought: How weird that my younger self identified as Sheila the Thief and not Dianna the Acrobat. I know which character I resembled more, though I guess my personality grew into the image my younger self had placed on me. For those unaware of, or just too young to know what I am referring to, there was once a mystical, magical fantasy adventure game, comic and cartoon named Dungeons and Dragons. Look it up – the cartoon version. I digress...

My brother, Barrington, had lived with my mother, who was not his mother, for nearly two and a half years and had attended primary school with my sisters. He was in the year below, my maternal eldest sister and the year above the other. His own mother had felt that he desperately required the guidance of our father at his age. Luckily, my mother was able to play the stepmother role to him at that point in time, which guaranteed him a much softer nurturing than the missionary discipline that would be instilled by my father's parental offerings.

It must have been good for my sisters to grow, even if only for a couple of years, with a male in the house – two males for that matter. I know for sure the dynamics would have been nothing like the termagant, feminist, coquetted, testosterone lacking environment, which I grew up in.

Over the years after he went back to live with his mother, he kept in touch with us and he and I would visit each other whenever possible. I remember my first solo trip to London to stay with him, his mother, little sister, and his huge dog. I was shocked by the size of their residence as it was much smaller than I was used to. My mother lived in a three-bedroomed house with an upstairs and downstairs, so coming to a London two-bedroomed apartment or flat was very different from my family living experience. That visit, Barrington's mum taught me about housing allocation for cultural minorities, the difference between the types of accommodations built in various cities and the basic reasoning for why this was.

I remember the constant feeling of secureness while being there. I grew close to Barrington's younger sister. Her birthday was days from mine, and we got on so well. One day I confessed how grateful I was for the experience of getting to know them and how great it must be to be her because she had our brother with her all the time. She embraced me lovingly and told me that she loved the fact that we shared a brother, that she was my sister too and anytime I needed her, she would be there for me. She made me feel that anytime spent without them by my side meant nothing at all because we would always be in each other's heart and thoughts, so distance became just a word. That day, I understood what family truly meant. There was no need for me to feel any ounce of jealousy or loss because his family were my family. Our little sister taught me to appreciate every sibling I have and from that day I pray for them all, whether I know them or not.

Barrington and I grew an unbreakable bond on that visit and to this day as adults, we still support and advise each other often on how to be better than we were yesterday.

This brother took the role of a model big brother with most of our siblings, attempting to cater to some of the void that comes from having an absent father. Barrington wasn't your classic role model but because he had fallen victim to some of the deterrent factors of the society we live in, his strength and determination to overcome the side effects of lacking parental guidance within our culture, made him the perfect brother for the position. He had such passion for us all to connect, so each family link would create a strong and sturdy chain for our children to grab onto along their future life journeys. Sometimes this would be to his own detriment, as each of us has had a different upbringing and because of that, his heart shines as solid gold to me as he never gives up on us. He sees in us that which I don't believe our father ever took the time to see. I am proud to say my big brother is a living lion, a chief and a warrior.

My father, I guess he is a lion also in his own right. He was a well-respected member of the Rastafarian culture/religion into which I was born. My mother was also a dedicated member spending much of her time assisting in many of the organisational bodies under its umbrella. There was a Music Body, an Art Body, and a Cooking Body, to name a few. Through my youth, it was in these locations I would have most of my interactions with my father. For a while, he taught in our Saturday School. His manner was extremely authoritative, yet still, he had the patience to ensure that you understood the teaching.

These days were powerful to the making of my identity and played a large part in my thoughts formed of men in my childhood years. They assisted in making my personal morals, and I guess they helped create my ideals of how men and women should and should not conduct themselves personally, publicly, and professionally.

We were taught about our cultural history, about those who had paved the way for our liberties today. We were taught about the African continent and the lineage from King Solomon to Hailie Selassie I. We read about speeches by great humanitarians. We were told about the way our ancestors lived before we were labelled by pirates as uncivilised. We were taught about the Rastafari goal and mission to repatriate. There were multiple hand-painted posters of aeroplanes and ships waiting to carry us home to the Motherland. The pictures were so full of hope and determination. Everyone was dressed in white Sharma with Red, Gold and Green Banners on their heads. Each person in the images seemed as if they were on a mission. Even the children looked as if they were excited to be in the waiting line for this journey. These pictures always gave me hope.

I used to spend a lot of time in the music studio there. I loved the beats and couldn't help dancing and singing along to those melodic rhythms. I loved the stories they told and the messages they gave in such clever ways, the poetry was inspiring. That's where I met Mr Denroy Morgan. I knew the words to some of the songs he practised, and he was in shock that someone so young found joy in the music he made. He promised that I would see him again before he left for his next tour destination. I was used to broken promises by then, thinking it was something that adults said to humour children when they wanted to leave them on a high.

When my mum called me downstairs and he was actually sat there eating fruit in my mother's good room, with the furry white rug – no children allowed, but today was different, I just screamed with glee. He had kept his promise. All men did not lie. I had met a male who had scrapped a phrase used by so many females around me, to justify their disappointment with the men with whom they had placed their trust.

We spoke about Mr Morgan's children, whom he had left at home in the USA. He showed pictures of them telling me how much he missed them when he was away on tour and that I reminded him of his daughter because she would sing with him and do his back up just like I had done. He said my smile was bright like hers, filled with sunshine. I secretly wished my dad missed me like that. He gave me an album on cassette and a huge poster with him smiling. My mum put the poster up on my wall for me the very same evening and I played that album non-stop for the next few months.

"Come join the people, let's all have some fun.

Universal party, come on everyone, let us have some fun.

Come on, come on people, there's no time to fight.

Ooh, it's time to come out of the darkness and into the light.

Come with me no fantasy, it's time to be alright.

Ooh, it's time to come out of the darkness and into the light,

let me hear you say it now, into the light...

We can make it happen, believe with all your might yeah,

Ooh, it's time to come out of the darkness and into the light.

If we join together, then love is in sight yeah,

Ooh, it's time to come out of the darkness and into the light."

My favourite song from the album which, of course, I rewound and replayed multiple times, to both of my sisters' distress. Then the tape cassette disappeared with not a member of my household knowing a thing about where it had gone.

Dad and his friend, whose home was like summertime, were chefs in the Cooking Body and sometimes cooked for the organisation's events and celebrations. The food was absolutely exquisite, and the meals served were always healthy in portion. The chicken was always perfectly seasoned and never fried dry, the rice was never too soft. Ital, oh my gosh, the Ital stew, delicious. I can taste the curry goat now just remembering how the gravy changed the colour of the rice, the polystyrene plate, and the plastic fork. Now that is perfect nostalgia because it's been over 11 years since I've eaten meat. There was nearly always reggae music playing except for when it was time for prayers and team songs sung by the whole congregation, with African drums and tambourines. Visitors could sing along too as there would be someone leading the verses by reading out the words before the line came like a vocal karaoke box.

Those events were the best occasions of my dependant years. We were all one ginormous international family with its own internal security. This felt so empowering while growing up in a country where hateful slurs and racial discrimination were spray-painted on walls and graffitied on public transport. It was a collectively mutual network who all shared the same aim. It meant that regardless of blood or race, there would always be an elder to look out for us. To assist us with whatsoever, we may need whether that be a plate of food or a session of reasoning for a better understanding of life.

Every so often, when my father would come to my mother's house, he would either bring along a sibling or take me to meet one or two, depending on accessibility. It amazed me at that time how I could only just be meeting them, especially as some of them lived in areas just beside the one I lived in.

Each time he came, he looked so very smart. Dressed in feathered Trilbies and Homburgs with Crocodile or Alligator skin shoes. Full three-piece suits precisely pressed with a seam almost as sharp as a blade in his trousers: embroidered satin or silk shirts and silk patterned or diamond socks. Thinking back, he had a very 1920s gangster theme going on. He never had any fluff or specs on his clothes and his shoes were always polished to perfection.

His executive cars were always immaculate. The wheels were jet black, body clean, polished, rims and windows shiny enough to show a true reflection. The interior would smell of forest freshness and remained prestige looking for the entirety of his ownership. It was clear he had expensive taste.

'Quality over quantity,' was always the phrase which came to mind, but this was a total oxymoron to me.

How could a man who loved quality so much create such a quantity of offspring yet give no regards to the quality of life they are given? A real-life oxymoron or straight selfishness, whichever it was, it made no sense to me.

I wondered if his mother had slept well knowing there were so many grandchildren which she did not know, I wondered if she knew she had so many grandchildren. I wondered if she even knew the actions of the boy she raised, I wondered if she had been the one to raise him. I wondered if she was the one responsible for his misjudgement of the female species. If not then who or what was to blame for his miseducation of responsibility.

He never spoke much of his youth, nor did he introduce me to any of his siblings. He'd said that he had siblings and I have since spoken to his sisters and one of his brothers, so I guessed he must have spent at least a small portion of his childhood years around females. Still, something must have gone drastically wrong during his youth or with his early rearing I concluded. That was the only reasonable explanation for his way of life. How could a man attract the heart of so many women and not want to treat them in a way he would want any other man to treat his mother or sisters? This was beyond my analytics. How could this man be so skilled at biblical verses and yet, not understand what an honour he'd been given by so many?

He did believe his sperm was of exceptional quality, though. He often bragged about the fact that he had created so many offspring, with all of them being as physically perfect as any parent could wish for. This he believed was a blessing from the Most High. I could not fault him for that. As far as I knew, this was true, but I could fault him for justifying his failures in sharing parental duties with biblical scriptures, knowing full well that there is always a scripture to default whichever one he chose to use.

I would question him about my siblings and why he had not introduced us all when we were younger. He would always refer to the mothers as being the chief obstacle for his attempts at doing this. How he'd tried so many times to arrange for us to meet and complications and animosity were the only reward for his efforts. I tried to explain to him that the mothers I knew had introduced all of their children to each other; and that he was the common denominator in all of our lives; therefore, it should be he who was responsible for uniting us. He would always avoid the continuance of the subject and deflect the conversation elsewhere. This would become a repeated topic of argument in my later life.

"What yea sow, yea shall reap."

You see, I grew up loving moral giving storybooks, my earliest favourite being, '*The Little Red Hen,*' you know where all the animals wanted to eat bread, but none wanted to take part in the chores necessary to create the bread. My father's concept of parenthood was far from in line with my beliefs on how it should or could be done. He sowed, oh he sowed alright, and a great many seeds at that, but he failed to tend his crops expecting that he would still reap the goodness of their wares.

I remember once during a disciplinary session, threatening to tell my father on my mother. She was dishing out the legendary 'syllable' beating, extended by her explaining to me that my father plays no part in raising nor responsing for my financial, physical, or emotional upkeep. From the food I ate to the socks on my feet, the only person on this entire Earth, maintaining my access to these things was her. The message I received then, as clear as the stinging in my skin, was that my father was good for nothing but procreation.

This began my analysis and condemnation of the male species.

There was a time I had had an allergic reaction to my, at the time best friend's new kittens. I'm giggling to myself as I write this because it seems so weird using that terminology now. Although we didn't often see each other at that moment in my life, Shonett was my best friend. She was the kind of friend where it seemed as if no time had passed since you were last together. The title of best friend would be passed between her and another childhood companion whose friendship is just the same. I really can't help laughing at how much we felt that title meant back then. I had stopped over for the night and had the best time looking after the new kittens, but I couldn't breathe properly when we woke in the morning. The last thing I remember is Shonett's mum telling me to keep breathing and Shonett's sister calling an ambulance. I heard the sirens, and then I was staring at the huge pore holes in the paramedics T-zone.

My mother had rushed to the hospital to meet us there. She didn't have much money on that day and by the time I was discharged, Shonett and her mother had left in their car, so we had caught the bus back home. It was quite a warm day, but I remember feeling so cold and very tired. My mum said it was the medication, making me feel that way and promised me some pampering when we reached home.

Along the walk from the bus stop to our house, I saw my father's car pass us and head down a street where another one of his friends lived. He stopped, turned the car around and parked in front of us. I cannot remember the full conversation which took place. Still, I do remember trying to plead that the attack I had suffered was not my mother's fault, being told to get into the car. My mother left to walk the rest of the way home by herself.

That was an unsettling point of awareness for me. I questioned my mother on the whys and what fors, of that happening. She gave me a piece of advice that I have passed on to my siblings over the years, "try to concentrate on YOUR relationship with him." I heard her at the time, but still, I was somewhat insulted that I had witnessed such brut callousness from my father, aimed at the only person in the whole world who had been there for me nearly every day of my life.

I got to spend quality time just once, which I remember while in my dependent years with my father at his Birmingham apartment. I was so very excited. My mother had agreed that I could stay with him for a whole week during the holidays. It would be me, four of my brothers and our dad. I was absolutely ecstatic! I packed my best clothes to carry with me and then my mum came and repacked my case with only two of my good outfits and lots of house clothes. I wasn't impressed. I contemplated attempting a negotiation with her, but I decided that it didn't matter because I was going to spend a week away with my dad and my brothers. Turned out that the case my mother had packed was perfect for the planned itinerary.

My father came to collect me, with one of my younger brothers and we were off. I was so happy as we pulled up outside of Edris' house. He was the only sibling I had met at the time who was deeply melanated. Because I too was a darker shade of dark brown, I found being in his company quite comforting.

While we waited in the back seat of the car, my younger brother asked if I had ever been to stay with dad, I shook my head and looked out of the window. I knew he had been before and was at the age where bragging might seem impressive to him. He did exactly as I had presumed and proceeded to tell me of the last couple of times he had visited. I had met this little brother several times before and although he was extra cute, he was so annoying at times. He would always brag about the time he spent with our father and though in my mind I justified this with him being male, his boasting still got to me and he knew it did, so he just continued. I blanked him out and continued looking out of the window, it was a warm day, so I pressed the electric window control and fiddled with the beads on the tail of my extensions.

The front door opened, and his voice faded into the background as Edris stepped out of the house. I could have burst with glee when he caught my eye and revealed his beautiful, white-toothed smile. He bounced towards the car and put his bag in the boot. His complexion caught my attention the most on this day. It was just as cocoa bean brown as I remembered but it had this lovely sunshine glow all over it.

Dad was red skinned with oriental shaped eyes. He grew his facial hair and had quite a long beard, but it was always well pulled and neat in a Rastaman, rugged way. I remember seeing a loc forming on it once and thinking, how did it managed to look so tidy still. I didn't think I resembled my father and when I looked in the mirror, I could never see what the people who claimed I looked like him saw, but when I was with this brother, I saw the resemblance.

We would be meeting up with two more of our brothers who were already waiting for us at dad's Birmingham apartment. I still recall that as being the one time, I really got to see the nurturing side of my dad.

The time we spent was so intimate, orderly yet homely and very humbling, to say the least. Interacting as a family with this section of my family was the total opposite of my usual living. Being the only girl there, my brothers treated me like a princess and I just loved feeling like one. Dad spoke pieces of his past and reminisced with us, he cooked for us, he taught us his moralistic values and told us of some of his cultural and spiritual beliefs.

We shared jokes and laughed together. My brothers spoke of their adventures with dad as he did of them.

It was beautiful and has remained the best memory I have of my father being a dad. He smiled so much during those three days. Yes, I said three days as the week was cut short due to other business. My brothers and I were delivered home and that was that.

The next momentous time I can remember my father being there for me was quite an episode. We'd moved to West Yorkshire. I made a few good friends, who remain that to this day. I also made a few life-enhancing acquaintances. Some of which never held my best interests at heart and were living, it seemed, only for whatever entertained them.

For example, I'd arranged to meet one of these acquaintances (who I thought to be a friend at the time), at the home of her brother, which he shared with Cleo, my mum's friend's daughter. We had planned to meet there and chill for a couple of hours after school.

Cleo had always been accommodating to me. Whether because of the family connection or because she actually liked me, she was always hospitable. She was like an older cousin to me, which I was ever so grateful for because I had not met any of my cousins who were living in the United Kingdom. It was kind of lonely, having no real aunties or uncles, so the ones I gained through family friendship were the next best thing. Cleo was younger than my older sisters. So it was probably easier for her to relate to what was being experienced in our teenage years. She would often advise us on some of the facts of life. We would go and sit with her now and again and help her out with her baby boys.

I remember the first time we met. My little sister and I had gone with mum for dinner round at her mum's house. As the visit had gotten to 'big people talk' and my little sister was playing outside, I was sent upstairs to introduce myself. I crept up the stairs, trying to remember which door I was told to knock. First on the left was the instruction. I knocked and heard a small voice saying, "come in...." I turned the handle and pushed the door, as she smiled, she reminded me of a young Tisha Campbell. I smiled back and told her my name. Cleo introduced her partner to me and told him to send his sister to meet me as she was the same age as me. He kissed her and left the room.

Cleo leaned up and crawled over her bed to give me a hug telling me to make myself comfortable. I noticed her swollen stomach. I instantly remembered how tired my sister had been once her stomach had gotten to that point of swelling. I congratulated her and asked if she was looking forward to becoming a mother. She told me that she was ready to meet her baby boy and caressed her stomach as it shifted and changed shape. She smiled again and we talked until Eliza entered about 20 minutes later. Eliza and I gelled straight away. We attended different schools and would often meet up in free time at Cleo's Mum's.

Cleo moved out of her mother's house a few months later and set up home with Eliza's brother bearing him another son. I watched his interactions with his children and how nice it was that the two of them still flirted with each other in public. It was a joyous sight to see. I didn't visit them as often in their home, maybe two or three times a month.

I must have been about 15 by this point in time and I looked forward to spending time with her sons. I read to the boys while Cleo ran their bath and when she took them up, Eliza lit the spliff she had rolled for us. We shared and conversed for a while, then there was a knock at the door.

Eliza jumped up to answer it and came back telling me that someone was there for me. Cleo, who had returned and was rising from her chair, looked at me and I shrugged, I wasn't expecting anyone. I thought this strange as this was not my house and though I was a regular visitor, no one except my friend knew that I would be there that day so who could possibly be knocking someone else's door for me?

It turned out that Eliza, my 'friend' (the term used loosely), had set me up to fight with a girl she had had a previous disagreement with at her school. I did not then, nor do I to this day, know anything about that girl, other than her being the sister of a girl who had been a member of a group, that were rivals to a few of my school friends.

The main and unexpected problem with this fight was that it had extended into an outright family street brawl within an hour. Sisters, mums, brothers, cousins, and even fathers were drawn into the chaos. I doubt that this was the outcome Eliza had expected, but effectively, our friendship was never the same after that day.

My father had made me secretly proud. I felt like he may have fallen short on the lovey-dovey stuff, but at least he was able to provide some sort of security for me when he was required to. He was at my mother's house within a couple of days to hear my version of events, as my brother had notified him of the word on the streets, regarding the episode.

Just under half of the youths in the area had turned out to watch the revelations, so the talk was a lot of truths, mixed with the many usual additions of gossip and Chinese whispers.

I'd heard that my dad had gone to the girl's father's shop and threatened to set fire to both, and the home of his daughter, before terrorising the rest of the family with his army of sons, if he heard any more on the matter. (Well, that's what I was told). My father himself never alerted me to exactly what he had done to resolve the issue, but people responded very differently to me after that.

My father was well known in Yorkshire, Manchester, and Birmingham. He was also quite well respected, admired and sometimes envied by way of his life path and the changes he had made, little did I know at the time; so his name carried recognition amongst the older generation. In actual fact, he was known in many UK cities, not a man short of petrol, to say the least.

The next couple of decades would pass with me seeing my father on occasion, sometimes more frequently than others, but it was always quite awkward, and the atmosphere was usually quite tense for me.

We were always very civil with each other. Onlookers would believe that we got on very well, as I was extremely respectful of him and his image. I feel that he too was mindful of the perception he gave to others, to be honest. I think there was always a void between my need to be desired as a daughter by him and his need for independence from his responsibilities.

In my adulthood, after seeing that my father was not budging on his thoughts and feelings about being the one to arrange our gathering, I began arranging get-togethers. It began with meals with the Northern siblings and then we connected with the Midland and Southern siblings. The title changed to reunions at that point and each time we have them, my soul sings and my spirit dances. The vision of our children playing together is one of the most beautiful displays my eyes have beheld.

The knowledge that we have changed things for them, that our children might have much more wholesome futures knowing who and where their family members are and that there is an abundance of love and support that exists for them anywhere, they turn.

Eventually, we'd like to have one with cousins, aunties, and uncles too, oh that would be a sight to see.

I remember breaking down on my father once while he transported me and my daughter, a young baby at the time. He'd never seen me cry, but I was so frustrated with his answers to my questions that I snapped and in the most respectful way I could, told him that he did not care an ounce for his grandchildren, because he had failed us and refused to introduce and unite all of his children. That was the first and only time I saw tears in my dad's eyes.

Our song: 'Should I ~ Dennis Brown.

Dolly House
Chapter Two

Primary school juniors we were. Kemar was the first boy to ever show an interest in me which encouraged him to spend his money on things he thought might make me smile. He was one of my class peers and we got on well. He was smart enough to have a decent conversation with and he worked well in groups. He'd meet me to walk to school in the mornings and buy me chocolate bars. My favourite was a Bitz, mint or orange, both flavours were just fine.

The boys in our class always seemed to have a problem with Kemar, but me and my friends were fine with him playing with us. He was always happy to help, pleasant and sociable. He was also really respectful to us girls which most of the boys had a challenging time with.

Looking back now, we must have been the nerds. We very rarely had excuses for not handing homework in. We worked hard on assignments and projects. Anya had the best handwriting of all the females in the school, including the teachers. Anya was a quiet, introverted girl with a complexion as dark, if not darker than mine. She was really clever, and we could talk for hours about things other girls of our age paid no attention to.

Looking back, we weren't as a group remotely interested in the things that were exciting our peers. Most of our conversation was educational or quizzical and we had no desire to break the rules unnecessarily. We aimed for marks above three-quarters of the possible total and congratulated each other on our achievements.

Kemar was a victim of peer pressure. Along with the racial profiling and community stigma mixed with cultural taboo, religious ignorance, and social unawareness. Jeeze, Kemar really did have himself a cocktail I wouldn't wanna digest.

By the time we hit year six juniors, he gave in to what would today be known as discrimination, and on Valentine's day, I was presented with a card and a note. Lucky me... not! The note read, Will you go out with me? with two answer boxes labelled, 'Yes' and 'No.' I watched as the boys all giggled in a huddle after I read it. They knew what it said and were waiting for my response. It took me nearly a week to reply. I didn't want to go out with him just because they had pushed him into asking, I was quite fine with our friendship, and I thought he was too.

The boys were pretty cruel to Kemar when they wanted to be, they would often bully him and call him names. They thought he was too sensitive and said he was overly feminine. I deliberated on how sad that must make him feel and considered what the boys would say if I said no.

I ticked the yes box and gave it back to him in front of a few boys for witness. He was so relieved, but I knew it was more about them being satisfied that he could get a girl, than him, actually wanting a girlfriend.

We commenced our primary school romance of holding hands and little peck kisses when required. My afterschool schedule was pretty filled so we only had the walks to home from school to spend time together and that was fine for both of us.

One day the boys were goading Kemar hard, telling him to touch my breasts if he was really my boyfriend. He gave me prior notice and awkwardly brushed his hand against my C-cup breast as we walked into class after break. The boys giggled but weren't satisfied with what they had seen and somehow, by the end of the lesson, Kemar had acquired enough courage to run past me, push me to a wall and squeeze both my breasts painfully hard. I was so embarrassed, in pain and really annoyed because boys were all laughing and propsin' him up about what he had done. Well, that was the beginning of the end.

We mutually decided to end our relationship after a couple of days when the taunts from the boys had died down. Kemar apologised and explained why he had acted so out of character. I forgave him after a couple of days of him begging with chocolate treats and we went back to our respectful, fun-filled friendship. Still meeting on the way to school most days and sitting next to each other for trips, our friendship was more than solid. We left primary school the following term and I was secretly relieved to be attending a school just for girls. Boys were idiotic.

I began high school. For the next two years, I was so pre-occupied with extra-curricular activities that I didn't even think about boys. My eldest sister was on her third pregnancy, and my mother had warned me off boys from I began high school. They didn't interest me anyway, so my mum had nothing at all to worry about. As much as I had begged her from the previous year, to allow me to go to a mixed-gender school, I was enrolled into a single-sex school.

I knew that females from my culture having complexions as dark as mine didn't get far in life unless they married well, had amazing talent, or were extra intelligent. I was multi-talented. I found it easy to learn new skills and adapt, and for that reason, I became intrigued with learning as much as I could. I competed with a girl in my class for the title of top in every subject, achieving either first or second place. I played the Flute and Timpani Drums as a part of the school Orchestra. I joined the Netball and Basketball teams and sang in the choir.

I was mesmerised by Science. Psychology being my most fascinating subject, since this area of study would define and explain the causes and actions of human behaviour. I also enjoyed Religious Education and History. Although, I found it exceedingly hard to place anything taught in History, on an accurate timeline, when none of what was being taught pertained to anything directly related to my culture or ancestral past. Whenever I would ask my teachers questions about the facts and how they pertained to a family like the one I had, it always brought repercussions of detentions and suspensions for, supposedly, disrupting the lesson. I quickly learned that in these subjects, first place was not going to be mine. I blamed this on the man who created the curriculum. It must have been a man because a woman would have been much more intricate and accurate with the details of her teaching subjects. That was my thought at the time.

I was in year nine when I decided to let a boy be my boyfriend, and it sounds crazy, but I only ticked the 'yes' box again, because I was leaving the town the following week and he said that me moving didn't matter, because he'd liked me for so long. It sounded pretty corny, but it worked. We had planned to have a long-distance relationship. He was going to call me twice a week and we were going to write to each other. I don't think he even replied to the first letter.

My song for Kemar: 'True Colours' ~ Cyndi Lauper.

In the Morning
Chapter Four

───────── ❧ ─────────

Teddy was my first proper boyfriend, my first love, my first true partner, and with him, I spent my first night.

After a tumultuous time in a new town, getting to know new people, it was a blessing to meet someone like Teddy, most definitely heaven-sent.

He was in the year below me in school and though most boys of his age were after exploration, he was different. Yes, he wanted to explore and do a lot of the things teenage boys do like play computers and eat, but he was more mature than most. His thinking was years beyond his age.

To me, Teddy had a soft and sensitive nature. He cared about feelings, he cared about the effects and consequences of actions. He had had much to deal with in his younger years and he had learned the art of making someone feel special. He sometimes reminded me of an older man in a much younger boys, well-fed body. We could have been something spectacular, but I was naive and unaware of the magnitude of hurt I could cause.

We were so good together that we could have been together forever, but destiny had other plans. He found me in a disturbed, messed-up state. I wasn't even aware of how mentally and emotionally tangled I was back then.

I was teased about the age difference, as most of the girls of my age were interested in college boys, or older men with cars. My Teddy was only five and a half months younger than me, but because of the way that the school year fell, he was in the year below me and others around us tried to make it an issue. We couldn't have cared less, though. We were happy in each other's company, and that was all that mattered.

He was teased for being with me. It had been nearly two years since the lie had been told and the rumours had spread like wildfire. Other happenings had taken over the limelight, but some people felt they could use this false information as a weapon against me. It meant nothing at all to me, but people can be cruel. As I had not reacted pleasingly to any provocation, they directed their defamation at him.

He asked me what had happened that day and promised that he wouldn't react badly to anything I was going to tell him. I took him through the day step by step. He held me close when I finished and calmly asked me to call William. He was getting tense, his body was becoming stiff, yet his hands were still stroking my shoulder so softly. I tried to explain that William had tried to help me and that he had suffered abuse from them too, but Teddy got so mad. He argued back, saying that he had seen William on multiple occasions with the same set of boys since then.

For a second, I thought about whether I had been used as a trade for popularity, but I quickly shook that thought from my mind. I remembered how he had looked that day. They weren't fake bruises, were they? I didn't want to think ill of William, and I didn't want Teddy to either.

He got up to leave, so I tried to block him. I was babysitting my little sister and couldn't leave the house, so I pushed shut the front room door as he headed towards it and threw my body in front of it. I pleaded with him to calm down and not start all this up again. I had gotten through the worst of it and I didn't care what people said any more. His nostrils were flaring, and he was starting to pant, I'd never seen him so angry. He threw me on to the sofa and left. I shouted after him, but he just kept walking, ordering me to get back inside. I screamed his name as I watched him turn the corner. I was having palpitations. I could feel my chest tightening up as I shut the door.

I didn't know what to do. Where was Teddy going? He could walk for hours, so I knew distance didn't matter. Oh, my goodness! What was he going to do? I prayed for none of them to be home. I didn't think at that time, God was watching over me, but he had clearly been on their side for this whole episode, so he ought to make sure my Teddy didn't find them. For their sakes if not for ours. Oh no, what if he went to Williams? His mum would find out, then my mum would find out, and then they'd ask why I didn't say anything to them. Oh my gosh. My mum would call my dad straight away. I started seeing blotches. I couldn't breathe.

I paged Teddy, over, and over again, but I knew he was way too irate to call me back. I called his cousin's home and left a message. I told him that Teddy had left in a temper and asked him to look out for him. All I could do was wait, and cry at what tomorrow might bring.

I ran a hot bath and went to soak. I had been crying for over an hour, and I felt mentally and physically drained. It was going to be, as it was going to be. All this time and now the first male

I really and truly liked, was digging up the worst thing to happen to me since being alive.

I was so mad at him, even though I knew he just wanted to avenge me. I worried about the trouble he would get himself into and what his family, especially his mother, would think when they heard. My head was spinning, shooting pains were firing to the back of my eye sockets. I had a migraine, and I had scrubbed my private area until I bled again without even noticing. I cried again.

The door knocked. "Oh, shit! Please be Teddy, please be Teddy." I silently pleaded.

I wrapped a towel around me and went to my mum's bedroom window. It was my mum's friend. My heart stopped. I told her that my mother wasn't home from work yet. She said she knew that, and demanded I open the door, so she could come in and wait.

"Oh, shit!!!" I opened the door and went back upstairs to finish washing off. I could hear her questioning her son, but I couldn't hear any replies. I was washing out the bath when I heard mum's key turn the lock in the door. "Oh, shit!!!"

My mum shouted at me to get down the stairs immediately. I didn't have any clothes on, and she did not care. I forwarded down the stairs, with a towel wrapped around me. She and her friend straight tag-teamed me, with a barrage of questions, so fast that I could not reply to any of them.

Teddy had gone to four houses and had found William at his Granddad's. The last clear question I recall was his mum asking me why I had sent my boyfriend to attack her son. I looked at his face. It was worse than it was on the day it happened. It was swollen, and his skin was broken in four of five different places. I told them that I hadn't sent my boyfriend anywhere.

My Mum got mad and dragged me by my towel. It fell free from the twist holding it in place and exposed the top half of my body.

"Ask him!!!" I shouted out, as I grabbed it back on.

His mother had brought his little brother along for the show, and he was enjoying it so much, all he needed was popcorn. I was so embarrassed. My cousin didn't speak, other than to say that he had told his mum to leave it. He couldn't even look me in my eyes. I asked my mum if I could leave the room.

William didn't tell his mother why Teddy had come for him.

He knew though, oh he knew exactly why Teddy had gone there, but the damage had been done and I guess all was easier left as it was.

I had a false reputation, but I was holding my own and so long as Teddy could let this go now, this mess of a so-called life could continue.

We had been dating for a while, Teddy was so sweet. He made me laugh when I was feeling low and always made me feel appreciated. He held me close and warmed me up whenever my hands got cold. He gave the best cuddles. His body was always at higher temperature than mine and he made me feel so snug in his arms. He was my protector, my partner, and no-one dared say anything hurtful or disrespectful to me when he was with me.

We attended schools on either side of the City Centre, so he would call me as he got in, after he greeted his family. We would talk for hours on the phone, about anything and everything when we weren't together and still have good conversations when we were. The amount of times my mother cursed me about the size of the phone bill. I would contribute more of my weekly earnings from my Saturday job to the household to try to compensate, though it always seemed unfair to me that I had to contribute anything at all as I was never in receipt of regular pocket money, like many of my friends had been since primary school.

Teddy had told me that he was given an allowance by his mother from his Child Benefit payments. My mother had a good job and worked most days, so I felt sure I should be receiving something. I did babysit my little sister for free while she was at work. I was now fulfilling the role which two of my sisters, several years older, had been occupying just months before. I attempted to approach the subject with my mother but was immediately shut down as I mentioned the word benefit.

Teddy would help me financially on occasion, unbeknown to my mother. Sometimes I was short on school fare, or I didn't have enough for snacks while we were chilling at his aunt's house. She was also an old friend of my mother, and she too was a member of our religion. She was always very good to me, serving me homemade desserts; her chocolate sponge was my favourite. She conversed with me about the general things a teenage girl should be able to address with an adult. Her daughters became like younger cousins to me and her family adopted me as another family member. I guess they too saw that what we had was special and could have lasted longer than time itself, if only destiny was to have allowed it.

He was ever so gentle and caring. Teddy always took the time to listen well and he knew how to show me his emotions, but he wasn't so good at speaking about them, especially if something had upset or annoyed him.

We both got on well with each other's mothers, which is a bonus for any teenager and all in all I can say that we had all the makings of a real-life teenage love affair.

I remember how nervous I was the night we decided to take things to the next level. We were going to reinvent the loss of my virginity, making it everything it had not been. It would be the remix, our remix. Thousands of miles better than the original and it was something that we both wanted.

Teddy had come to see me an hour before my mother had set off for work and had left just before her. She was on night shifts at the nursing home, which had been the norm for a while. Her husband was the responsible adult in our house.

Note, I call him her husband because he never tried to get to know me nor my little sister. It was more like having a lodger than having a stepfather. He used to drink quite heavily and would pass out, wherever he devoured the deciding number of canned lagers to his daily demise. Responsible was the incorrect wording, just adult will suffice. His presence is like a glitch in my life story. He was neither then, nor what I would class today, as a decent man or worthy match for my mother.

The scene was set, I had put my little sister to bed, read her a story and listened to her say her prayers. After telling her goodnight, I ran a bubble bath and soaked for an hour. Then, I made my way to my bedroom, which was on the second floor in the attic, stripped my bed and changed the sheets. After sprinkling the bottom sheet with a little talc and spraying the pillows with perfume, I flopped onto the bed. I had a classic 1990s slow jams mixtape that Teddy had made for me playing. I began to ponder all the things that might hinder our plans.

My mother might return home early, but that was highly unlikely. Her husband may catch us on Teddy's entry. That was highly unlikely too. He had managed to work his way through the whole four-pack of Super Tennents, so that was a real silly thought. Teddy's aunt may not allow him out of the house, who knew what excuse he would use. I told myself to rest my mind and went to the dresser to style my hair and practise sexy faces in the mirror.

I got the call and went downstairs to unlock the door. We crept up the two flights of stairs like ninjas, his steps echoing mine till we reached the top of the house and entered my bedroom.

The moon was full and high. Through the skylight in the sloping roof, we had full view of its entire magnificence. I turned the lights out, and we lay on the bed, his arms firmly enveloping my waist. We gazed out of the window and began to count the stars in view. We exchanged smiles and kissed...

We woke early the next day, we had only slept for a couple of hours. I was in his arms still. He stroked me tenderly and kissed my neck. He knew where my weak spots were. I could feel his stiffness knocking on my thigh. The house was silent apart from my mum's husband's snoring. I reached over, pressed play on the ghetto blaster and we snuggled under the sheets for a very good morning greeting.

Things between us seemed to be even sweeter after that night. He called me an hour after he left, to let me know he'd gotten in without alerting anyone to his absence. We chuckled and spoke for the next two hours as if we hadn't woken up together just hours before.

Our remix was so far from the original, it was a different song altogether, and I loved it! I loved him for giving me that night. I loved him for giving me value again.

The devil don't like happy!

My mock GCSE's were coming up and I was steadily revising, sometimes with Teddy's assistance. I was smoking Ganja to keep me calm and trying to concentrate as best I could. I still had demons haunting me, though, telling me I wasn't worthy of a love like that. That I was tainted, spoiled and one day he would believe the same things as others, who heard false rumours and spoke without clarification. The voices in my head were so very loud that I just could not focus. I knew nothing about depression in those days. Although I felt that something was not quite right, I just unknowingly continued to suppress it, thinking that I was doing fine. There's always someone worse off than yourself, was a frequent saying in our home.

I had gone to top up on my self-prescribed mood enhancer, Madam Mary J. On my route, I bumped into a mutual friend of ours.

I had met Jermaine a few months before I met Teddy, and he had expressed a keen interest in me. He had questioned me several times about becoming his girlfriend. He'd waited for me to finish my work one Saturday, so that he could walk with me home. He even introduced me to his mother, but this interest he had expressed for me wasn't exclusive, so I didn't care to further our friendship.

Teddy had been grounded for a month after being involved in a fight at school. It would be sod's law, if that fight was in my defence and knowing my luck, it probably was. We had limited talking time and were not permitted to see each other when either of us was grounded. Teddy's mum was more lenient than mine and we knew if he kept his head down, we'd be fine by week two or three. This was the second weekend and Jermaine suggested we go to his house to listen to some music and smoke one while taking a break from studying. I had about three hours of study time left before collecting my little sister and I was going to have a smoke before getting back to my books anyway, so I thought why not.

Errr... so from this point, you can guess what happened next, can't you?

We talked, smoked and listened to some mind-blowing tunes. It's funny how in my adult years listening to the same songs, I realise how much I was both aware and unaware of at that age. SWV's 'Downtown' was in that selection. I know, now that it was a different kind of downtown that I imagined at that time in my life, I can tell you that for sure. I was oblivious to so much back then, I have to laugh.

We smoked some more and talked about our future aspirations. One more spliff and we had taken ourselves into a dangerous zone. I had ghosts crashing through my thoughts of happiness and I was missing the only person who could keep me grounded at the time. Here I was feeling fragile and overly horny. Teddy was always there when the memories intruded my thoughts. I could call him, and he would talk to me until my mind was cleared of them. If we were close, he would hold me and kiss me, or cuddle and comfort me. Being close to someone who cared for me vanquished the fright and fear that was bubbling and boiling away inside of me. He knew exactly how to make me feel secure and he always did whether it was in person or by telephone.

I was listening to all the best mind seducing tunes of 1994, with the guy who missed the shot, telling tales on his friend who had caught the ball. I should have taken my black ass home.

But I didn't. We shared another spliff, and one thing led to another.

I immediately regretted it because I knew this would not go down well at all. Shame shadowed my every step home. Why did I do that? What had I just done to my life? I had betrayed my partner. I had betrayed the bond that we had, and I had broken his trust. He didn't even know. Did he know? Could he feel what I had just done? I felt like he could. I had allowed uncertainty into my meditations and opened the door for Teddy to become distrustful of my loyalty to our love. My actions were full of immaturity. I gave in to the feelings of unworthiness, committing adultery or teenagery as was the case.

I called Jermaine that evening, just before my scheduled call with Teddy. I told him that what we had done was wrong. He agreed to my surprise, but then he went on to tell me how strong his attraction was to me and gave me an ultimatum. I couldn't have been more stunned. He told me that he could not get me out of his head and that he felt that he had betrayed his friendship with Teddy. I confessed that I couldn't leave Teddy for him and begged him not to say anything before I did. Jermaine agreed and left it with me. I didn't think it was right to tell him over the phone, so I evaded the subject until the next day, as his mother had lifted our contact ban.

Jermaine had gotten to Teddy before me. They attended the same school, and all-day my nerves were on edge because I just knew that the day's energy was bad. This left us in a position I could not physically comprehend. There was nothing I could say or do to erase my actions or its effect on the holder of my heart. Teddy couldn't even look at me anymore, and when he did, his eyes glazed over.

He displayed doubts of me so fiercely after that and was unwilling to move from the stance he had taken on his insecurity about me and my actions. I found his rejection so challenging that instead of fighting for what I knew to be right and correct, I chose to walk away after trying to change his opinion of me for a couple of months.

It was as if everything we had grown to be, was a waste of time. I convinced myself that he would change his mind if we were meant to be, and he would want what we had back again before long. I went to his cousin's home unexpected, in attempts to persuade him to talk things through with me, but he refused. I ambushed him on his way home from his grandparents. I even stalked him all the way home one day and he told me to stop wasting my time. So, I eased up, calling him less and less.

After six months of his cold responses, I concluded that it wasn't to be and maybe I had left the pot to simmer dry, metaphorically speaking. I induced myself with thoughts that he would be better off without me, he would be better off with someone closer to his ideal.

The ice he gave me was just too much for me to cope with, I just felt frozen and numb. Mixed with the guilt, I felt for giving in to this sordid need for intimate contact and the cocktail of dancing demons giving me constant public anxiety; I fell to the mercy of a suicidal attempt to bring it all to a halt.

I pray one day he will find it in his heart to forgive me for letting our fairy tale disintegrate. I was weak in mind and spirit, and I did not know what a mess I was creating.

Our song: 'Didn't We Almost Have It All'
~ Whitney Houston.

NB. I am aware that I have skipped a chapter, but all will be revealed later.

Daddy Issues
Chapter Five

───────────── ∿ ─────────────

JD was my older man. Eight years my senior, he had his own apartment, his own cars and his own bottle of charm.

We met through introduction by Stephanie, a mutual friend as he was her Mary J supplier, soon to become mine too, we would see each other around three or four times a week. Small conversations soon became stimulating flirtations. The more we smiled with each other's brazenness, the longer our meetings became.

One day JD asked me on a date, I had little or no hesitation in saying yes. I wasn't yet 16, but I had left school unofficially because it was examination time. I was only required to be on school grounds for the days my exams were scheduled. He wasn't especially attractive although his eyes were a lovely shape. He didn't have the best body either, in fact, his body was miles from the best. It was more like chubby or extra padded and because he wasn't very tall, it was very visible. I didn't mind that though, he dressed well enough for a weighty guy, and he had intellectually intrigued me. He was comedic, confident and considerate enough, for the chase. Stephanie had boasted of his loyal friendship and encouraged the union.

I did have one thing plaguing me, though. I couldn't remember if I'd told JD my age. I figured it must have come up in conversation at some point but couldn't be sure. I had to find a way to break it to him before the date. I saw him twice before the date. Both times, I got so carried away trying to be the better flirter, that I didn't know how to tell him without it making the previous chatter sound sordid. I finally built up the courage and called him three hours before the date. He asked if I'd rang to bail out and I took that as my cue.

"Did Stephanie tell you I'm not 16 for another three weeks?" I asked full of confidence that if it were a problem to him, at least I knew I was on his radar. He knew my age, and it wasn't an issue as he only wanted to get to know me, he assured me. The date was nice. He smiled a lot, and I just kept on saying the stupidest things. I was so nervous, but he was aware and did his best to ease the tension with jokes and compliments.

I left home just days after my 16th birthday. The relationship between my mother and I had hit a dead end. Endless comments about me wanting to be a woman before my time; two bulls living under the same roof and assumptions that my life's goal was to destroy my mother's sanity, had worn my tolerance to string thin. After being grounded and restraining my mother's attempt to discipline me the old-fashioned way, I took her up on her order to leave from under her roof. I packed a bag and opted for sleeping on Stephanie's sofa for a couple of weeks until I found lodgings in a family house that Latisha, Stephanie's friend, was lodging in. It just so happened to be the same house where JD and I had first made acquaintance.

I felt somewhat betrayed by my mother at the time, for thinking she knew me better than I knew myself. It had been years since she knew me. She was antagonising over what I could be doing, without ever actually knowing, or taking the time to observe what I was doing. JD tried to remain neutral on the situation. I thought he may have been safeguarding his living space. Although it would have been nice for him to offer me residency, I didn't want him to do so under these circumstances.

We dated for nearly ten weeks before he asked me to stay over at his. I wasn't sure if this was a compliment for him to have restrained for so long, or if I just wasn't attractive enough above the gossip that had been, years before. Either way, I was content that he had waited.

I was in no way prepared for how JD wanted to love me. Before I had spent the night, JD had told me a few things that he claimed he did not want me to hear from anyone else. He told me he was confiding in me because he cared a lot about me and wanted to be honest with me. I found this so appealing and respectful, I can't believe how naive I still was.

He had told me of his journey to ghetto wealth. How he had a few girls working the streets for him in Bradford, three to be precise and the amount in kilos of illegal substances he managed to move each week. I say ghetto wealth because, make no mistake, this is not the same as wealth in dictionary terms. Ghetto wealth is the ability to buy what you want. It allows you to help out certain members of the community financially or influentially, but the owner of this type of wealth rarely has any assets which will not be seized, should they ever be held in HER Majesty's free residence for an extended period of time.

I remember him dropping me home after telling me this. He said he was giving me time to process the information so that I could make a clear decision on whether I wanted to commence a relationship with him. I didn't call him the next day, and by 8 p.m. that evening, he was calling my phone. He was inviting me round for a Chinese after I finished work the next day, accompanied by a conclusive conversation on where our friendship was going. I felt sure he was treating me like an adult, and I wanted to keep this feeling.

I agreed to meet him the next day and continued to mull through the situation in my mind, in the meantime. This man was doing the same things I had heard, through several grapevines, that my father had done years before him. I was a product of someone who had lived a life very similar to this, so I ought to understand that people can change. He had told me all of this of his own accord, and it was now known information. Something that nobody on road could tell me and surprise me with. I had the upper hand, and he had given it to me. This man must want me for the right reasons, I convinced myself, and a week later I was spending the night.

A few months into the relationship, I remember cleaning his flat one day and finding an appointment card. It wasn't for the doctor's surgery, the address was in the town centre, it said Genitourinary Clinic. I thought it sounded like maybe there was a problem with his urinary system and figured he would tell me if it was something for me to be concerned with. After all, we were having an adult relationship. He had been honest about his earnings. He had even taken the time to get to know me, so I was sure that this was nothing for me to be worried about. I placed the card on the top of the television in his bedroom and proceeded to the kitchen to make lunch.

Now you have to think back. This was a point in time when we used pagers. Cell phones were as big as breeze blocks, and we weren't even calling them mobiles yet. There was no Google or Siri for me to consult. Nokia 232 had not long been introduced, and JD had two of them. I had no clue what Genitourinary meant and JD had given me no reason to doubt him up to this point. He never spoke to me about his medical issue, but I would soon find out exactly where that appointment card was from.

I was 16 and two thirds when I experienced my first pregnancy scare. Initially, upon missing my regular monthly, I was appalled. I wasn't ready for this. JD and I had been together for nearly eight months, we were living separately. He wasn't doing anything to show any progression of our relationship, other than being more possessive, which wasn't enough to make good parents. We hadn't even gone on holiday together yet never mind bringing another life into the world. Ahhh, the beauty of the young mind.

When I told him, I was late for my period by nearly three weeks, he hit the roof. He was fuming, telling me that I had trapped him and that this was my intention from meeting him. He ordered me to get details for an abortion, give him the bill and not try to communicate with him until I had done so. I told him to go and 'four-letter word' himself. By the end of his rant, I had decided that I was keeping this baby, and he would regret saying any of those words to me.

Three days later, his flat was raided, and he was imprisoned for a short spell. He called me on his second day, but his mood was the same, he just wanted to be rid of our creation. Twelve days after that, while attaching a weave to a client's head,

I experience the most excruciating pain in my pelvic area. It was so bad, I folded into the foetal position. I called my doctor immediately for an emergency appointment.

It was much easier in those days to get a same-day slot. On this occasion, there was an availability 20 minutes from the time I called. Thank God, I thought as my client hurriedly drove me to the surgery.

The pains got worse and the twisted, wrenching feeling was deeper. I knew what was happening and all I could sense was guilt for not wanting it when I initially found out. Had my thoughts penetrated my womb and caused this to happen? We pulled up outside the surgery, I went in and took a seat in the waiting area.

At least my mother who had, now moved back to Manchester would never be shamed by the friends of hers who had told her that I was staying in West Yorkshire because I wanted to, 'tek man.' She would be none the wiser and neither would they. JD too would be happy with this result, much to my dismay.

The first month after that was filled with ashtrays, alcohol, and work addiction. By the third month, I had begun a new relationship. That one didn't last long at all. By the second month into that relationship, I'd had a visit from the police, I had fought with Latisha, I had fallen out with Stephanie and a gunman had crept around to the back of my house ready to pop him. Luckily, this man knew me through one of my brothers, so, as I opened the patio door, that gun was tucked straight away but, I also found out that he was snorting more than Porky. I am a born Rasta, who has never had a fondness for pigs. I knew all about how desperate addicts can get. By way of the energy, he had brought into my life in such a short time, I had full confirmation that he was no surety for anything but stress.

The demons were back, and I was fighting hard to keep them at bay.

I began to chill less and less with Stephanie and Latisha, although we had resolved our issues. I spent more of my free time with Halle, a friend I had made from school and her crew. They had made me feel like an extended member of their family and still do today. I'd say it was them who assisted me in being ready to explore the Reggae music scene again. I started going on nights out with them and for the first time since moving to Yorkshire, I was feeling joyful inside and having fun.

Everything happens for a reason.

JD had sent letters and messages asking for me to visit him. He was apologising for all the things he had said, the way he had spoken to me and how he had made me feel. I took him up on his invitation. Prisons were nothing new to me, as I had been visiting my older brothers in detention centres and prisons from years previously. Nevertheless, I asked one of my good friends to make the journey with me. JD knew nothing of the miscarriage, and this was the first time we were exchanging words or seeing each other face to face after almost 20 weeks.

He looked clean and solemn in his overalls and oh, did I miss him.

Who else was going to hold me the way he did? He may not have been a saint but better the devil you know, was my analogy at the time. I had attempted moving on and had been placed into a direct life-threatening situation. It was better that I went back to JD, I thought and that is what I did.

JD was cheating on me within a year of us being back together. As I passed my 17th year and eighth month, not six months after he had left his cell, he was embarking on enticing a younger female. I'll refer to her as the 16-year-old.

I could not believe it. Why was he doing this to me? I was nearly 18. He had been in my life since just before I had turned 16. I had worked since I was 13 and at that time, I was holding down two jobs consistently. I was much more mature than most girls of my age. I had my own flat. All the people I socialised with were older than me, so it couldn't be maturity. I could cook, I could clean. I could dance and I had a banging figure now. I didn't get through a week without being approached, whether by males or females, so why on earth was this happening to me?

Maybe I was too mature for him. Maybe it was God's way of telling me that he wasn't for me, but I didn't heed that, not for a good while.

I finished with him upon finding out that he had had relations with this young girl by stalking him from a very close vicinity.

A break away from him and finding out that he had knowingly treated himself for a sexually transmitted disease, which he didn't even bother to alert me to, even though he was attentively exposing me to it, didn't keep my stupid ass away from JD. I say knowingly because it had hit me at the GU clinic when they handed me the same appointment card that I had seen several months prior to that in his bedroom.

I had all sorts of things going through my head. That filthy bastard! He could have warned me months ago! Was he sleeping with his prostitutes? Had he continued sleeping with me within six weeks of me finding that card? Did he know that he was putting my life in jeopardy? Did he know that harm he was causing to my fertility organs? Did he even care?

Regardless of all the facts, JD had convinced me that we were ride or die. I knew the worst of him, and he would soon experience the worst of me.

We got back together after a month or so, but it wasn't much better. We'd be good for a while and then he would become emotionally unavailable. After seeing that I had drawn the attention of a Sargent in the Navy, he became even more possessive. My admirer had driven clear from Portsmouth, to put a face to my voice. JD had seen his car parked outside of my apartment and sent a message with some young boys, advising my visitor that the wheels on his Bentley would be missing within the hour if it was found anywhere in or around the area.

He tried to be more attentive to my needs but avoided any deep conversations after that. I knew he was devoting his attentions elsewhere. I'll never forget one time when JD had removed me from a Blues party early one morning. I was dancing with someone at the time and JD was not impressed. He dragged me out by my arm and put me in the passenger seat of his car. I noticed that he was driving towards my residence.

He lived just up the road from the house where the Blues was held, in the opposite direction to the turn he had made, so I questioned why he had disturbed my dance when he was obviously intending on spending the night with somebody else. JD refused to answer every question I asked. He got out of the car and walked towards the main road. I sat for while thinking to myself. He'll be back soon. I tried to rewind the last few minutes of our communication. Did he say, he'll just come for it when he wakes up? Never. I lit the tail end of the spliff I had pocketed during the dance that had been rudely interrupted and waited.

I sat there for another 15 minutes, he did not come back. I thought about it all for a while and then I had a drunken epiphany. I enthusiastically took to destroying each and every panel of his car's bodywork, in a mad, intoxicated rage. It wasn't his only car, but it was the one he had spent the most time working on. It was his favourite car, so I knew it would anger him. I just wanted him to feel the frustration I felt for him, and with each slash of the screwdriver through the smooth white finish, I laughed a hearty villain's laugh. I remember thinking how pretty the many silver streaks looked as I ran swiftly past it, to my places of refuge the next afternoon. There was even a solo game of noughts and crosses on the door panel. I'm sat here belly laughing at the memory as I write.

He was not amused and spent the day hunting me down at every friend's house, that he knew the address of. I couldn't face going through the motions with him again, so I left that night for a few days in my hometown, with my older sister. The few days turned into over six months looking after my youngest maternal sister.

My mother had chosen to leave Yorkshire and return to Manchester a couple of months after I had turned 16. I refused to go with her, as I had begun a new life of my own. I had not wanted to live in Yorkshire in the first place, so I wasn't following her back there, not now that my future had been altered so badly. She'd chosen to embark on a six-month tour and was intending on leaving my little sister with a friend of hers. I did not approve at all and stated this by leaving my three jobs (well two), in order to be my sister's guardian until our mother returned.

I needed the space from JD, and he needed to know what he would be losing if I left. My friend was looking after my flat and I would be back every other weekend, to work the third job I had secured, bartending at a City Centre night club.

One of the return weekend visits saw me a little over-intoxicated at a house party. I had been told by several people that the same 16-year-old, was now spreading gossip about me. She was claiming that I had lost my puppy fat by indulging in A-class drug use. Apparently, that was the reason she was having to take care of my man's needs. I couldn't understand why she still had my name in her mouth, as I had been out of town for at least three months by this point. She may well have been tending to JD's peenie panting, but I had not once ever taken Cocaine nor any other A-class drug. My weight loss was purely due to me cutting back on snacks, dancing and partying hard three to four nights a week for a straight year. This is by no means a recommendation for a social diet, but I was young and that is what I did. I had even begun seeing someone closer to my age in Manchester, so she had no reason to even be thinking about me. I usually didn't even listen to hearsay, I had grown a thick skin because of it and refused to be a sheep but, that night I was so liquored up, that I must have grown wool through my drunken pores.

Anyway, it just so happened that she was at this house party I attended. I dragged her outside and let her know exactly what I thought of her loose tongue and invalid behaviour towards me, over a man who cared for nobody but himself. (I did not use those exact words).

He would not try to save her if I chose to cause her great harm in that moment. He would probably have turned and walked the opposite way if he had been there. I thought about how selfish he was. I thought about how stupid I looked at that moment. At the same time, I heard a male voice asking one of the onlookers if I was attacking this young girl over a man.

How embarrassing!!! I let go of her arm and walked over to the wall of a garden a few doors up. This wasn't me. I didn't enjoy this double-edged sword of embarrassment. Regardless of the reason I said I was at this party, it was because of JD that this had happened. I was cursing this girl because she was talking foul things about me, but she was saying these things to hurt me for his sake. I was attacking her over a man. In that realisation, I convinced myself that I didn't want him.

I attempted to pay more attention to the future I wanted. I completed my Touch-Typing certificate, also my Business Administration NVQ's I, II and III. I found a job at a City Centre hotel during the remaining three and some months of my guardianship. I impressed myself with what I could achieve when I didn't have a man taking up my time and sucking the life energy from me.

Things had not worked out with the guy that was closer to my age, as he showed me exactly why I had gone for maturity in the first place. He wasn't sure of what he wanted in life and I needed, so desperately, to be with someone who was.

Upon my return to Yorkshire, within the month JD had got to me again. I must say, it was refreshing to be in his company again after so long. He'd shaken off some of the weight he had been carrying and was beginning to get some definition. When he hugged me, it felt nicer than I remembered it being. When he held me, I felt as if his arms were the only ones that should be placed there. He spoke to me with the same firm but humble manner he used to use with me and his voice, oh his voice had me wrapped in ribbons. I was wondering why we had split at all.

Probably another red flag right there! X's are that for a reason, when we use Y for their return, Z is sure to follow.

JD somehow convinced me that he was no longer messing around. He claimed he had called it a day with the 16-year-old, from before the party weekend and assured me that I had no reason to feel insecure about his feelings for me.

He offered me a car upon finishing my driving lessons, I wanted him to pay for them, so this meant that the offer was not about to be adhered to. Silly little naive me could have been driving within the year, but this is how my mind had mapped it. I wasn't about to accept this conditional offer of a car when I could just as easily have sold my surname for eight grand and bought my own. The only reason I hadn't done so, was because I still held onto this illusion that marrying for love was so much better than a marriage of circumstance, even though,

What's Love Got to Do with it, the Tina Turner story was one of my favourite films. For all that I had been through with JD, I thought it particularly mean of him not just paying for a crash course of lessons if he was going to buy me a car anyway. He made more than enough money to do so, and I had paid my own way throughout our time together. He never bought me gifts and never gave me money freely, so I felt it was an insult for him to be putting any kind of condition on anything he was offering me. I had accepted little from him and now he believed that I ought to be as happy with a dangling carrot, as a hungry bunny.

He had even promised to introduce me to his mother, whom I had not yet met, even though he had met mine plenty of times. I thought this was a way of cementing his commitment to me. What a load of codswallop. I met her by chance one day when I bumped into them at the Halal butchers. He introduced me as his friend, my mistake, his good friend and that was supposed to count.

So, we were coasting. Things could not be said to be brilliant between us, but JD had been putting extra effort in lately. He was cooking now and again and returning to mine if he finished his working day early. We were almost in a routine. Then came the day of the Christening.

The baby being christened belonged to Latisha. She and I had been housemates twice. I still hold her as one of my truest friends, because after our falling out, she had met me in the middle to resolve the matter and preserve the respect we had built for each other. JD was to be the baby's Godfather and Stephanie, his Godmother.

JD and I had made no arrangements for us to travel together, but he had left mine early that morning to prepare himself at home. Stephanie had told me that she and her boyfriend were getting a lift with him. I thought it weird that he had not mentioned it but didn't let it play on my mind. I rode in a taxi by myself to the church and when the service ended, I called the same taxi for my return journey.

I had noticed that Stephanie's younger sister had also gotten a lift, but again, I thought nothing of it. After all, they had known him longer than I had. He had remained close to them throughout the years and he also had a friendship with their mother, so it was like he was more of a family friend. In writing this, everything seems to make a whole lot more sense than it did then, but the penny wasn't dropping for me at that time, no matter how loudly it clanged with the floor.

JD decided to create a scene outside of the church because I did not want to ride with him. I figure his alert was raised to my appearing to be without a partner. He hadn't given a thought to how I had gotten there, but now, quite possibly because he had observed that I was getting attention from other males attending the ceremony, he wanted to make it appear to all, that I was taken.

I had a weird indescribable feeling that day. I hadn't spoken to JD since exiting his car outside my apartment block. I knew he would be at the reception, so I figured we'd just get through this celebration and deal with it another time.

Later that evening at the reception, I got a nauseating feeling in the pit of my stomach. Stephanie had been a little offish, and although I knew a fair few of the guests, I just was not comfortable at all. I asked JD to drop me home. He was sat in the front room with a glass of Jack Daniels in his hand. He pointed at it, laughed and told me that he had been drinking and so couldn't drive. For the second time that day, JD was acting on-edge and out of the ordinary. I kissed my teeth and told him to leave the drink as it would wait until he had dropped me home. He raised his voice, drawing attention from the guests stood in the hallway. I think this was my first ever out of body experience. Within a split second, I was standing outside the front room window peering in. I could see JD as clear as day, waving his arms, pointing at the glass in his hand and the liquor in it swirling rapidly. I could see people in the hallway staring at someone, but it wasn't JD. I looked towards where their eyes were directed and saw myself stood there in disbelief. I jumped back into my body instantly, said farewell to Latisha and left the reception.

I couldn't contain my emotions nor the tears that were falling from my eyes. Something wasn't right, I had no idea what it was, but I knew that something just was not right.

That night I decided that I had to leave, not just JD, I had to leave the me that I sensed I was becoming. I had to leave the town and start afresh. I saw my future with this man. He would continue to cheat on me and because I had gotten with him so young, I would keep believing his excuses and go back to him. He would have babies to other women and then have some with me, to persuade me to stay and I would. I would be having babies, in between the many that he had elsewhere and spend years trying to make him see that I was 'the one' all along. I had seen it all before and could not resign myself to living that life.

I left that very next day. JD had been calling and I had ignored him. There was nothing more I wanted to hear from him. I had followed my intuition and he was not going to talk to me around this time.

I found a job in my old hometown and within a fortnight, I had moved, leaving my friends, my hopes for a happy ending with JD and my fully furnished flat. I asked Trudy, one of my friends in Manchester to do the round trip with me and she honoured my request. I returned for a few hours to tie up some loose ends and left, taking only what could fit into the back of her little blue Ford Fiesta.

All that happens in the dark will eventually come to light.

It turned out that JD had impregnated Stephanie's younger sister, not just once either.

I was far down a different life path by the time I found out and I was extremely thankful that I had listened to my gut. The Universe had given me so many warnings and red flags about this man, and I was like a bull, chasing after all that red.

Our Song: 'Eyes (You Never Really Cared)' ~ Gwen Guthrie.

A Fresh Start
Chapter Six

───────── ∿ ─────────

I had a new flat, was working two jobs and enjoying my new life. I'd reconnected with those from my past who had remained my friends while living in Yorkshire and I was ready to date again.

Levi had asked me out a couple of times and I had told him that he would see me again if it was meant to be. He surprisingly tracked me down. He came to my place of work and asked me out on a date. I was flattered, but when I asked his occupation, he told me he was currently unemployed. I told him he needed to have a job and some prospects before he approached me again.

Gosh, I was young and so very full of myself. I remember how confident I was at that point in time. I was feeling free and unfettered. I wasn't about to be taken for granted so soon after liberating myself from, what I had deemed to be, the long introduction to a lifetime of hurt and regret. The next man to get me into any kind of relationship would have to prove that he wanted me. A few weeks later, he had a job at a Shipping company, and he attempted to gain my company yet again. This time he was successful.

We had only been dating for a few weeks, but something was off with the situation. Levi had told me he was lodging at his cousin's house while waiting for his boiler to be fixed. I took him at his word, but my gut was doing its thing again. I decided to call it a day between us after a couple more uncomfortable phone conversations. One of them had an older child speaking in the background, followed by a total switch of the subject. Then the next found him abruptly disconnecting the call mid-conversation.

You got this, I thought to myself. I don't need to be around all that suspicious behaviour. I thought that I had caught a lucky quick break, but I was a date too late.

Two weeks later, I was late on my cycle again. I was feeling nauseous at night and in the afternoons, getting dizzy spells and migraines. I knew I was pregnant. I prayed for the outcome that most suited my life plan when I took the first pregnancy test. It came out positive. I took another just to be sure. It came out inconclusive. I was bewildered and booked an appointment with my GP.

Could God be doing this to me again? Levi hadn't even attempted to contact me since I'd ended things. I was sure he was trying to deceive me in some way. God knew the truth, so would he set me up like this all over again? Maybe this was different, maybe this was not a repeat of the lesson I had lived for the past three years.

The doctors' test took two days to process, but I knew what the outcome would be. My colleagues had told me to be mindful when making my decision. I was on my way to getting a mortgage, looking for houses and apartments with my friend. Keeping the baby would put a halt on that happening as money would need to be allocated elsewhere. This may be my only chance at this, I couldn't afford to take that gamble. Time was on my wrist, not in my hands. With that said, my choice was whittled to one.

I bumped into Levi in a local chip shop about a week later and called him outside so that I could inform him of the predicament. He asked what I had decided and arranged to come see me the next day.

Over the next two weeks, Levi confessed to living with his older woman and her children. He also confessed to her that he had pursued and been involved in a short relationship with me. He told her that I was pregnant and made no arguments when she asked him to leave her home. I guess he knew I was a bit of a soft touch because he turned up at my flat with a black bag full of clothes and requested my spare room for his stay until his boiler was fixed.

After a couple of weeks trying to gain his way into my favour and my heart, I agreed to try and work at being a family.

It was nice in the beginning. He was so romantic at times. I would come home from work to find flowers on my bed and chocolates under my pillow. He massaged my feet when they swelled and rubbed my back when the belly became heavy. He maintained the flat's cleanliness on days I was too tired or sick to do my share and he did his best to cater to all of my cravings. He'd drive for miles ensuring I had the exact fries I wanted or looking for the only brand of sweeties that subdued my heartburn.

We shopped together, watched football matches at the pub together, rented movies and went for meals together. He introduced me to his friends and his family, and I did likewise. It was really lovely. I wondered if this was it. Levi hadn't intellectually intrigued me, but I thought then that our union was for something which did not require much academic intellect. We were doing the grown-up thing. Destiny had decided that we were going to start a family. This could be me all settled now.

Levi had another side to him though, and from the day I saw it, our relationship was doomed.

I had returned from a long weekend visiting my friends in Yorkshire. It was fun to reunite with them. We often spoke on the phone but being with each other and everyone making time to be together despite the distance, was always a special factor for me. Upon my return, my girlfriends and I had much to talk of about the week's events.

I was in the living room, laughing and talking about how JD had become so jealous, he was counting down the days to the end of my pregnancy. And saying, without thinking, that we hadn't been intimate, for over eight months. I was only five or six months pregnant at the time, so this was highly amusing for us.

Levi had been listening in from the hallway and had misconstrued the whole conversation. He muttered and mumbled, calling me out of my name as he paced up and down the flat. I went to start ironing, trying my best not to respond. He was calling me all sorts of derogatory female abusive names. I told him that if he felt so little for me, he should 'four-letter word' right off; as I never asked him to be here. He was so angry I just saw his fist coming towards my face. My immediate reaction was to hit him back with the iron that was in my right hand.

Again, I was talking to the lord. Why would this man that had lied and deceived me want to do this to us when I was carrying his child? It wasn't even a fair fight. He knew how much this pregnancy had drained me. He could see that I was swollen with water retention from carrying all the extra weight he had given me. He could clearly see his child growing and protruding through any item of clothing I wore. Why was this happening? How could he do this to me when I had been nothing but obliging to him?

His explanation for the change of character was that he thought I did not know who I had impregnated me. He thought he heard me saying something about counting months and that the baby could have belonged to my ex.

That, right there is what happens when you eavesdrop on half of a conversation! This man had played a game of Chinese whispers all by himself.

Levi was eight years my senior. I had expected so much more from him. He had not even bothered to speak to me before winding himself up.

I had given him my trust after he had proved himself untrustworthy. The fact that he had gone so far to make right his wrong with me, and he had been honest with his ex and had humbly waited for me to be okay with him again, confused me even more as to why he would want to jeopardise what we had over an assumption based on a half-heard, misconstrued, conversation that was not meant for him.

We broke up for about a month with Trudy, his father and my father mediating between us. Levi begged and pleaded my forgiveness and promised he would never lay his hands on me again. He did though, once before we finally ended the relationship once again after we had been over for a number of months.

I think my depression kicked in again around that time. I began feeling worthless to everyone but the baby inside of me. This baby needed me to protect it, to feed it, to carry it. This baby needed my blood, it needed my mind, and it needed my heart to keep beating.

I gained more weight, I craved more weed, and I slept as much as I could. Life didn't hurt when I was asleep, and I felt like nothing more than a living incubator when I was awake. This man did not really love me. If he did, he would never want to see me hurt the way he had hurt me. He wouldn't want to see me bruised or bleeding and he wouldn't have put our baby in the dangerous position he did when he raised his hand to me.

Labour day came, Levi was at work, a couple of my Yorkshire friends were over for the weekend. All three of us were pregnant and in different trimesters. I remember how hectic a morning it was. I had been sick throughout the night and the Braxton Hicks were coming stronger and faster than they had before. I had chosen to have a Domino Birth Plan; which meant my midwife would deliver my baby whether we were at home or at the hospital, barring any emergency. I had rented my TENS machine and thought it was time to start preparing it.

The friend in her first trimester, walked with me to the telephone box about three minutes walking distance from my house. It took us nearly 20 minutes to get there and back. My eldest sister was who I had chosen as my birthing partner, so I called her also. She called Levi's manager and asked for him to be released from work for the day as his baby was on its way.

The midwife arrived about ten minutes after my sister, who was followed swiftly by my mother. I couldn't take all the fussing and begged for a bath. The pains were sharp, and the TENS machine was just irritating me during my contractions. The vibrations were doing nothing to ease the pain, so I ripped the belts off and headed for the bathroom. I felt sweaty and stuffy; water had always made me feel better. I climbed in and jumped right back out. The water was freezing. The midwife warned that it couldn't be too hot as it may harm the baby, but I needed more heat in this water, or I wasn't getting in. My mother ensured the bath was good for me to sit in, even if only for five minutes, which is about how long I lasted in there before getting out to vomit and to excrete what felt like, every last bit of food in my intestines. My eldest sister has spent many years reminding me that it wasn't.

Six pounds and six ounces was the weight of our beautiful baby girl. Her eyes were so shiny and bright. My first words to her were, "Oh my goodness, you have such beautiful eyes, I'm so glad to finally meet you."

"Daddy's Little Princess!" was Levi's introduction to his daughter.

Levi and I adjusted easily to parenthood with the help of my mother and a few friends, but we struggled to reinforce the crack that was now becoming visible in our relationship. We were sleeping together every night and waking together every morning, but we were not solid. He professed his love for me even more after Labour day, but I no longer trusted him. I wouldn't allow myself to feel anything more than I already felt for him. I was besotted with our daughter and while Levi may have seen her as my gift to him, I saw her as a gift from God and he was just the dark angel who had been chosen to deliver her to me.

I had lost faith in men. They had all let me down, up to this point. I was willing to accept that they were indeed good for, only, one thing; making babies.

He was an excellent father while we were together, and I could not fault him for anything regarding his daughter. Levi took her for walks, carrying her in the sling when she was still too small to fit in her pram. He dressed her, played with her, sang to her and spoke to her non-stop, he even spoke to her as she slept. Levi made promises to her that, had I known what the future held, I would have hit him with a Dutch pot right there and then. He was loving his role as a family man and it showed.

We held a beautiful family christening for our baby girl, exactly six months after her birth. It was attended by over a 150 relatives and friends. It was an epic. Food was ample as numerous family members from both sides offered their services. The venue had a bar for those who wanted more than the three bottles of wine provided for each table. Levi had arranged the music and entertainment. And although I spent most of my time in the kitchen, the few times I exited, all I could see were smiling faces from wall to wall.

We had done it; we'd pulled off an event with both our families. There was no fighting, everybody ate, drank and enjoyed themselves, and things were getting better between us.

Levi adored his daughter so much. He woke with her on a night, giving me extra, much-needed sleeping time, by feeding her with expressed milk that I had prepared. He took her on shopping trips and visits to his friends. He drove or pushed her round the block at teething times when she found it hard to settle. He was so good with her, and I was content enough to think about the possibility of nuptials with him.

Even if I didn't love him the way he loved me, he was doing alright as a partner and even better as a father. Sex was quite satisfactory. I had a high sex drive, and he was able to match it and more. He couldn't cook very well, but he was willing to try, so maybe I would teach him one day. I enjoyed cooking anyway, and he was glad to eat and wash up afterwards, so that was just fine with me. So long as I didn't make him feel like he had reason to be paranoid, we would be fine. After all, this had been God's plan, or so I thought.

The drunken mistake

That's what he put it down to, but I felt he must have known what he was doing because mistakes like that just don't happen. He had blamed it on the wind in his first excuse then, that it was an accident. Skirts in that material don't blow easily and how do you accidentally lift someone's Lycra and Viscose skirt?

Due to the person whose skirt it was, I just couldn't switch my view on this predicament. He would never find an explanation good enough to justify his actions. I wasn't prepared to take any more excuses and demanded him out. I didn't want him to be the first thing I saw on a morning, because the images of the possible outcomes to that situation kept swirling around in my mind right the way through the nights.

I thought about how he always told the people we met while out with our daughter, that she was not his first child. His first child had not survived premature birth, and he was still experiencing the heartache of that loss. I had told him how uncomfortable this had made me feel while I was pregnant. However, I had begun growing a little resentment towards him when he continued to do the same after she was born.

We had to split up, it was the only way. He wasn't considerate enough of his actions, and for all that I was doing to alleviate his insecurities, he had just added more to my list.

I would raise our daughter as a single parent if needs be, but I was not allowing this man to disrespect and discredit me any further.

This led to my next battle with depression. I began to feel unworthy all over again. Paranoia kicked in. I felt vulnerable and apprehensive of so much more now that I had a daughter. I had to protect her from everything and everyone in this world that wanted to bring harm her way. I was petrified at having to do this on my own.

I agreed to share contact with Levi. For a year after we separated, he maintained steady habitual contact with our daughter. He would keep her on weekends first, then this changed to fortnightly with nights in between. We were civil with each other, getting closer and then distancing as time went by.

I couldn't let go of the images in my head and knew there was no hope of a future with that kind of fungus growing under our bridge. It didn't matter how much water passed underneath it, that fungus would remain.

In the years following, Levi not only fertilised this fungus but added a dump truck of plastic refuse under our bridge.

I was forced to take out an injunction against him after an attack on my home. In his attempts to gain entry he had damaged my door preventing the lock from working and so my door locks had to be changed. I lifted the restriction after we began communicating in more of a co-parenting manner.

One evening after we had returned from taking our daughter to a photography shoot, we got into another violent episode. This went from a conversation to a domestic so rapidly. It began, us sitting in opposite chairs and escalated through the hallway, out the front door and into the cul-de-sac. It ended with our daughter hanging onto my neck with her toddler-sized fingernails; me being bent backwards over a car bonnet, and a young teenaged boy charging through a group of spectators at the pedestrian opening of the cul-de-sac, to wrestle Levi off me. I couldn't even stomach looking at Levi at that time. I took another injunction out against him.

Emotionally, my whole being had been shaken by this. I had always said to my friends that no man could do that to me. I had been the idealist, believing that men only did that to the women who allowed it. I had not allowed this, yet it had happened, and although I had fought back, or attempted to defend myself, it had still happened. Something about me had attracted this behaviour, something that I could not see. Something made these men feel that they had the right to treat another as a possession. I have never thought that to be the correct word as a possession something of value. Being treated like this did not display the intention of any valuable thought. It made me feel unloved and unworthy. Incapable of pleasing, a disappointment. It made me want my big wooden childhood wardrobe back.

I compared it to the discipline I received as a child. My mother struck out due to frustration. Frustration of not being heard or adhered to. Frustration too, of having to bear the full responsibility of child-rearing. A man that meets a woman of independent age does not have these burdens. The woman has already reached an age of capability enough to be consenting to the adult acts being entertained. She is not in need of discipline in this manner. Somewhere, the comprehension of how to relate to other adults for many males in this type of situation, is warped. For these men attracting a partner who can both, nurture them and meet their need for love, comfort and sex are confused with their thoughts about the role of a father.

At this point, I decided that only a man who knew the definition between the two roles and displayed good comprehension of them would be permitted within the nurturing circle of my daughter's life.

A few years later, he took me to court with his new partner to claim that I could be described as an unfit parent due to my mental illness. Levi was aware that I had suffered with post-natal depression and that I had been prescribed medication. Levi was unaware that I had rejected the medication and was studying person-centred counselling. I had also completed my Counselling NVQ'S I, II and the Diploma. I provided the usher with my certificates for the judge. This proved to the courts that I was aware of how to address any signs of the depression reoccurring.

It was said that I had prevented him from visiting his child. Yes, I had stopped him from legally being able to come to my home, but I had never prevented him accessing his daughter. His father used to come and see her, and so did his cousin. He could have asked any of the relatives, mutual friends or Godparents, that we had chosen for our daughter, to be an intermediary for his access.

All of these actions were done through the negative side of Levi and that was the side that had broken us in the first place, but more time would soon pass, and Levi would forget any parts he played in altering my view of him. He would deny any knowledge of the participation in my memories of his Mr Hyde personality. He would deny recollection of his actions, so far as to shatter any fragment of trust I ever held for him.

Unbeknown to him, this denial would create a wall under our bridge, so filled with stodge that the water would become totally stagnant.

For our child's sake.

We do talk, and by the time our daughter reached 21 years of age, he had rebuilt their relationship, which makes me smile. It took a lot of time, patience and forgiveness for us to reach the 'civil city' where we meet now. Ours was another one of those relationships where things would never be the same again.

However, it's better to be standing on a bridge over stagnant water, than not to have a bridge to stand on at all. Many times, I wanted to set our bridge alight. It would have been such a pretty bonfire with all that build-up of non-biodegradable material stuck beneath it. That action would not have assisted my daughter's future so that match was never lit.

Our Song: 'Thank You' ~ Jamelia.

An Act of Commitment
Chapter Seven

He was my other half, my forever, my Mr Right for me, or so I had thought. I had felt it too at a point; the only man who had gotten a, yes, straight away in answer to his proposal, with no words in-between.

It was expected but unpredicted at the time it arrived. It was romantic, embarrassing, adorable, very public and comedic. You could have almost described it as a well thought through performance. Everything I would never have asked for, and it worked.

We attended a Blue Mountain Theatre Production with his younger sister and parents to celebrate their anniversary. Speaking through a mic positioned in the lead actor's wig, after congratulating his mother and father on securing their Pearl anniversary, he called me up to join him on the stage.

I still remember, my legs going jelly-like and sinking into my seat, telling myself that he wouldn't embarrass himself by attempting a proposal here. His sister and mother helped me to my feet. I made my way through the row of occupied seats, everyone excitedly getting up and helping me along to the aisle.

I inhaled straightened my back and steadily strode towards the stage knowing the cameras were now on me. I was petrified and somehow confident all at the same time. One of the actors helped me up the stairs making more jokes for the audience, and Ray-Jay took my hand. He held it so gracefully as he got down on one knee. He told me how lucky he felt to have me in his life, how much my loyalty had meant to him, and then he asked me to be his wife.

Ray-Jay had been a friend since college days. I still remember how annoyingly irritating he was when we first met. So full of confidence that I thought him quite obnoxious to be around. It wasn't until I took my girls to a house belonging to a DJ friend of mine (Teddy's cousin to be precise), to practise singing that I saw another side to him.

He came around with his friend to rap and intelligence flowed from his lips like a talking encyclopaedia. He had such good use of poetry, positively constructed within whichever topic came his way. I found this very intriguing and saw him through a different lens from that day. We had gained a mutual respect for each other, and our friendship began to take its course.

We used to chill together purely as platonic friends. I had a boyfriend (JD), and RJ was a huge flirt with intentions to enjoy himself if nothing else.

My boyfriend was visiting one of Ray-Jay's neighbours quite often. Though there were rumours of his infidelity, I still found myself in shock when I saw his car parked outside with my own eyes. RJ convinced me I should wait until he had entered the flat before approaching, it seemed logical, so I did. By the end of the confrontation, I decided I was single again.

Unawares to RJ, he had signed himself up for a night of watching me turn from angry female friend to slobbering mess on the sofa. I was drinking fluently from liquor to cider and spilling my heartache until my words were no longer coherent. What a sight I must have been, what a night he must have had, but he lent his ear as I needed and did no more than hug me in my distressed, intoxicated state.

That night cemented our friendship for the two decades it lasted. He hadn't taken advantage of me when I had provided the perfect situation for him to have a field day. I was upset, feeling neglected, high, or extra inebriated from the weed, and drunk, hiding from the life that awaited me at home.

As the friendship blossomed, we found out that he was cousin to my eldest sister by my mother. This was a shock, but as there were no blood ties between us, we didn't see any problem with our friendship extending to a relationship.

Our first attempt was awkward, to say the least. It lasted about two months if that. I had unknowingly contracted a sexually transmitted infection from JD. Ray-Jay disclosed this to me in the most compassionate way possible. I felt sordid and disgusting. I wanted him to turn his view from me, I was totally repulsed by my being at that moment. He made sure I knew that it was not a fault of mine, that these things happen sometimes. I had done nothing but be faithful to JD at this point this definitely was not asked for. He assured me that it wasn't the end of the world and that nothing would change between us.

It did though, and for good reason, I might add, because I don't think either of us was ready for one another, until several years later.

Our friendship was sturdy and remained so for years. Through relationships, including me getting back with JD, relocation, a pregnancy and rehabilitation, we managed to rekindle our spark and were engaged to be married a decade later.

I was about seven months pregnant living in my hometown. I got a call from Ray-Jay telling me he was travelling to my side of the country with a mutual friend and they wanted to see me. We met at a local pub and he rose to greet me as I waddled across to the corner where they were seated.

We both hugged, as did our friend and they commented on how much I was glowing with my pregnancy. I was huge. About three sizes bigger than I was when I last saw them, and we all laughed hard when I told them it was okay, to be honest. We talked, ate lunch and then they returned to Yorkshire. I wouldn't see Ray-Jay face to face for another two years as he was incarcerated for three and a half years not long after.

I had contacted his mother after I got word of what had happened to him. She was quite shocked to hear from me but remembered me from the years before. It was nice that she recalled who I was. I expressed my sympathy for her and her husband being placed in this situation.

You see of all Ray-Jay's friends, he was the least likely to have a criminal record. He was never in need, thanks to his parents and he was intelligent and quite well educated. I imagined it must have been heart-breaking to his mother and she was such a lovely lady.

I asked her to send the message that I would like to visit him, if he would allow me to. I knew how things went when young men were locked up. The friends that claim to be by your side and to have your back are nowhere to be seen, once that cell door is shut on you. Prison is a lonely place for anyone but especially for a young black man with Christian or Catholic, Caribbean parentage.

Ray-Jay's parents stood by him firmly and were there for him every step of his journey back to the life that they had worked so hard to provide for him. I was welcomed into their home like a long-lost family member. His little sister became my little sister, and my daughter gained an extra set of grandparents.

A visiting order dropped through my letterbox and I arranged my first visit. I visited Ray-Jay monthly. We wrote to each other and he called me weekly. After a few months, his calls came nearly every day. We went from being friends to falling in love with each other.

When you write, you speak from the windows of your heart. There is rarely shame in disclosing the view and because of this, letters can give the sincerest thoughts and feelings, a transient breath of life. Reading becomes a conversation of minds, and imaginations are given space to run free. Expressions are much more elaborate when written. There is an honesty that comes easily, a version of you that springs up when a pen or pencil touches paper. As if your mind and soul are communicating harmoniously by way of the script.

Ray-Jay was quite well built, around six feet and two inches with the most beautiful eyes. Being in prison just gave him the time and tools to perfect the boxer body he already had, and oh my gosh, did he perfect it. I tell you he couldn't have been carved any better than he was, and I was the only unrelated female getting to see all of that fineness.

I was so excited when he got his home visits, as were his family. He was too, but it took him a little while to adapt to existence back in the world again.

Looking back now, it must have felt like a whirlwind when he came out. On top of him having to adjust to being a part of a society that had moved on without him, he also had to take on the role of father, full time.

Just a few of weeks after he was fully released, his 11-year-old son, named Mario, turned up at his parent's house with the police. Mario had left home insisting that he did not want to return. I guess this altered Ray-Jay's plans immensely. He now had to cater to his son's needs and live at his parent's home while doing this, must have emasculated him quite immensely.

I began looking for property to mortgage in Yorkshire, we had discussed my moving back and agreed that it was doable. I had not long received an inheritance from my grandmother after she had passed away and what better way to invest in my future. It seemed to me that Ray-Jay's mother was more interested in my return than he was, as she ended up doing the majority of the house hunting with me.

Ray-Jay finally confessed to me that he didn't think it was such a good idea for me to mortgage in Yorkshire and I backed off. I didn't want to make him feel he owed anything to me. It was my choice to be with him while he was incarcerated, and my choice to wait for him to be with me. The last thing I wanted was for him to feel obliged to be with me.

After Levi, I couldn't trust men, but Ray-Jay was different, and I didn't want to change the way I saw him. He was the only one that had proven trustworthy of all the males I knew, and I never wanted him to feel like he ever had to lie to me to spare my feelings.

We continued to visit and call each other for a short while and then one day he said he wanted to move in with me and my daughter instead. I got straight onto finding a school for his son. Mario was due to start secondary school, but had been excluded from every primary school he had previously attended. Ray-Jay struggled to get him into an educational setting that didn't remind him of the judicial system he'd just left. I registered him into a school for boys. I hoped to avoid giving them his previous education records until he had settled into the school properly. Hopefully, they would see him as an asset to the school if I could get him to behave himself, while he was there.

I purchased his full uniform and bought any school equipment he required for starting. A neighbour of mine had a son, a year older, who was attending the same school, so they met and travelled to and from school together.

It took just under two months of family get-togethers, cooked family meals and attending parties together, for this bright young boy to start drawing pictures of family picnics, as opposed to the Grim Reaper pictures I had found lying around the house when he first moved in. He was enjoying his life and had told me so.

Mario was greeting me with hugs when he got home from school. This was a far cry from the angry little boy that had chained himself to the bathroom door, weeks previous. His grandmother had noticed the difference in his attitude and outlook also. Never before, had he been exposed to this concentrated type of closeness, inclusive of him and I could not have been prouder of his elevation.

His school teachers highlighted his skills and he was looking and behaving much more confident in himself than when he first came to live with us. We were decorating his bedroom, which was the first and only bedroom he had had to himself since his sisters were born. I allowed him to pick out the accessories to his Football themed room. He was absolutely overjoyed.

My daughter was five years old and had always had her own room as she was an only child, but I had shared a room until I was ten years old, so I knew how he felt. He now had full responsibility for a whole room, and everything inside it belonged to him.

It had been about three months, and Mario asked if he could visit his mother's home to see his sisters. He missed them so much, and he was being such a good big brother to my daughter.

I had to convince his father to allow him a visit as he didn't think it wise after such a short time, but I had managed to talk him around. I so wished I could have taken that back, but everything happens for a reason.

Mario's mother had become jealous of the life he was now living as if it were detrimental to her existence. She told him that Ray-Jay was not his biological father and totally destroyed Mario's current and future happiness. I couldn't believe she could be so cruel to her only son and first-born child. Why would she want to play with his mental health like that? Surely, she should be proud of the improvement in her son's conduct and attitude towards life.

Mario was so distraught that he would not speak to Ray-Jay when he went to collect him. He shouted what he had been told from the bathroom window, accused his father of lying to him and claimed he did not want to live with us any longer.

Ray-Jay was devastated, his parents even more so. For 11 years, they had all nurtured, loved and cared for this child, to then be told that he had no connection to them was the saddest thing to witness.

Ray-Jay became distant with me. Mario's mother was blocking his calls, and he had lost the spark about him. Just as he was starting to move on with his life, weeks later, we got a call from his parents. Mario had turned up at theirs after walking nearly 16 miles from his mother's home. They had fed him and were awaiting our arrival.

Thank God, I thought. My prayers must be getting answered now. I had hated seeing Ray-Jay in so much pain, and I had blamed myself for convincing him to allow Mario access to such a vile woman, regardless of the fact that she was his biological mother.

She had made such a mess of raising him, and she had felt nothing but envy at her son being able to live a stress-free life without her constant manipulations. She had lost her babysitter, her butler, her protector and the one male who would have her back regardless of how badly she treated him. Her behaviour was that of a manipulative, spoilt brat rather than that of a mother of four. It was as if she felt Mario owed her a debt of gratitude for existing.

I can't stand that type of parent mentality, it absolutely sickens me. For her sake, I prayed that I never crossed paths with her while her son was still a minor. She had given pain and heartbreak to two generations of family. I tried to take my mind off her for the rest of the drive up the motorway.

We got to Ray-Jay's parents' home, and we all hugged. I missed Mario, and it was clear that he missed being with us. He looked so rough and unkempt. He told us that he would not go back to his mother and that Ray-Jay couldn't make him do so. The police had informed us that they had been contacted by Mario's mum, and she had told them that she did not want him to come back to her house.

Ray-Jay was stressed, but I couldn't figure out why. We were good now. Everything could go back to the way it was eventually, but that wasn't the case for Ray-Jay. He had been so wounded by the way in which the revelation came out, and he was deeply offended by how Mario had spoken to him.

You see Mario had met his biological father during the time that we hadn't seen him. He had further verbally abused and disrespected Ray-Jay by comparing the material gifts that his new, real dad had given and promised him. After a few visits with his new dad, he had begun to see that he would never be treated in the same way as the sons to whom this man had been a father from birth. He had started questioning the differences openly and obviously did not appreciate the way this truth was given to him by his new dad.

Ray-Jay insisted Mario's mother's wishes were followed and explained to the police that he did not feel he could take Mario back as his son, after all that had happened. His parents pleaded with him and even offered to take him on themselves, but Ray-Jay refused. He also felt that Mario living with his parents would strain his own relationship with his parents.

The officers explained that the only option they were left with was to place Mario into the state authorities' care. Ray-Jay agreed to this happening. I was shocked and disturbed by this. This behaviour was foreign to me, and to what I knew of Ray-Jay. I told him he could not leave Mario to just go with strangers and if he felt what he was doing to be right and correct, he should be the one to hand him to social services, not the police.

It was the least he could do, since this whole decision had been made by him to safeguard his feelings and not that of the innocent 11-year-old boy. He did as I asked, and the hour-long drive back home was mostly silent.

I tried to support his decision but found it incredibly hard as I really didn't understand. I think I may have nagged him a bit because it didn't sit well with me that Mario was with strangers and his bedroom was sitting empty. Ray-Jay broke down to me one afternoon not too long after.

He confessed that he had known from birth that Mario was not his. He had even gone as far as to have an argument with his mother when she questioned the paternity of the baby.

He had carried the guilt of that for all these years, and now, here was karma slapping him in his face. This explained everything. The reason he couldn't face Mario living with his parents even though he himself only visited twice a month. The reason it would put a strain on his relationship with his parents and the reason that sad little boy had now after 11 years, been abandoned. He was punishing this boy for actions that had been taken by him when Mario was an innocent little baby.

I was gobsmacked. How could Ray-Jay do this? He had allowed me to become attached to a stranger without informing me. He had deceived me into living with a child that had absolutely no connection to anyone I knew. He had put our whole friendship and relationship in jeopardy, and he didn't even know it or maybe he did.

The proposal came not too long after this and was quite a surprise to me as we were not at our best when he chose to do it. For some men, marriage was a lifeline. I figured he wouldn't have cherished the thought of me turning him down in front of such a mass of people. He had to truly love me to risk leaving a memory like that on his parent's anniversary.

We made initial wedding plans within the next year, kept an engagement party, and took a UK break together.

Ray-Jay was becoming distracted where our relationship was concerned. I was putting on weight and had gone from a size ten on the date of the proposal to a comfortable size 14 by this time. I knew my weight gain was an issue and was assured of this by photos I found in his phone of women posing in underwear. It was quite ironic, looking back. He had actually sent me into his phone to retrieve pictures from a recent family trip we had made to Alton Towers, and the provocative photos were right beside them. He had ranted about respect for his privacy, yet I did not know the code to his phone as he had opened it for me.

Until that point, I didn't even consider that Ray-Jay was dividing his attention for me. We were doing all of the things that couples supposedly do, and I honestly didn't even acknowledge other males. They were all just other people once I had accepted that ring. I guess that may have played a part in the problem. I was no longer available, so my focus was working, cooking and being at home with my family. I paid no attention to my becoming less attractive to him, as he, with all of his enhanced self-inflicted flaws, was still the man who I had said yes to. He was the man I was ready and willing to forsake all others for. I guess I had fooled myself into thinking that he felt likewise about me until then.

Parenting became an issue for us because I wasn't getting pregnant. We had been trying for a while and nothing was working. On one occasion he had even described our intimate time as a chore for him. We went to the doctors and were referred to the hospital for fertility tests. Ray-Jay thought that he might be the problem as I already had a child, but I think I was the problem.

I had developed polycystic ovaries and three small fibroids in my uterus. I so badly wanted to give him a child, and I was still carrying a small amount of guilt over the whole Mario situation. If I hadn't persuaded him to let Mario go, that whole episode might never have existed.

Things were strained in our relationship again. Money was becoming an issue. The inheritance my grandmother had left had depleted, so had the five grand loan, I had taken from the bank. Ray-Jay decided to change careers and take a job he had been told about in Europe. We talked on the phone daily about our current and future plans, and we were planning to relocate in Italy. That was until Shabnam became an issue.

Shabnam was Ray-Jay's work colleague from his previous job. She had left her job at the company after a few sick notes from her doctor. She had been claiming to be addicted to marijuana. I didn't think that an excuse like this would reflect well on her future employment chances and had shared this with my fiancé. Nevertheless, Ray-Jay had taken it upon himself to recommend her for a job at his new workplace. I thought this a bad idea. It would be a derogative reflection on his work ethic should she decide to use the same medical excuse again.

I had previously expressed my upset at this friend becoming too comfortable with him. She was wearing much less than she was when I had met her, swapping her religious, fully covered garments for western wear. She was now a liberated Muslim, with makeup, tops showing her midriff and she followed

Ray-Jay everywhere she could. I would find evidence of her being in my home while I was out assisting with my brother's after-hours alcohol delivery business. Now, I would leave after 10 p.m. and return after 3 a.m. on the nights my brother asked for help, to paint a picture of why I grew so weary of their relationship.

I told him I was not happy about what he had done and asked him to withdraw the job referral. The very next day, I received a call from Shabnam, but she was calling from the same number Ray-Jay used from time to time. She was telling me I had no reason to feel vulnerable by her working in Italy with Ray-Jay.

Really? I had no reason to feel any way in jeopardy of my partner, my future husband succumbing to her femininity over 1300 miles away from where I was standing. I was absolutely livid, and I threatened to burn down the house, she was renting a room in, if she did not return within the next three days. Ray-Jay called me back fuming, telling me I had no right to speak to her in that manner. Shabnam left Italy two days later.

Ray-Jay returned the next month. I hadn't been taking his calls as often and felt we should probably just wait until we were together again to talk about us, if there even was an us to talk about. I stopped looking for schools in Italy, took off my engagement ring and continued as best I could as independently as I could. I felt so disrespected by the two of them. Ray-Jay apologized for his actions. He said everything I wanted to hear and convinced me he was committed to me by proposing again in private. This time his promise was to prove that he was the same man I had fallen in love with.

We were planning wedding again. It had been a few months, and much to his mother's relief, we had chosen the colours, decided on the wedding party, started the guest list with parent allocations and pinned down a date.

I had been trying dresses with my friend, who was also engaged. We had both found our perfect dresses. The weight had dropped off and I was almost back in a size ten. I went to place the deposit on mine and couldn't resist trying it on again. It was totally different from the one I had initially set my heart on, but I looked absolutely, stunning. The material draped around my waist, clenching it at its smallest point. The layers of satin which fell flawlessly over my hips towards the fishtail at my calves made me feel and look like a 1950s movie star. My figure looked unreal, it was the best I had ever seen, but something felt wrong. I left the dress shop with a purchase of a necklace and earrings set for my mother's birthday, and the deposit still in my purse.

Two days later, we had decided to have date night at home. Ray-Jay went to buy some Cognac and I prepared myself in sexy lingerie in wait for his return.

I got out of the shower to hear his phone ringing. It had been ringing a few times, and I thought it might be from one of his Italian contacts, so I decided to answer it. I would never usually answer his phone unless he asked me to. I have no interest in seeing anything not meant for my eyes, but he had been expecting an important call, so I went for it. The screen said Polar Bear, so I thought it must be a work colleague as we knew nobody with that name. The voice that replied sounded too familiar. It couldn't be, could it? He wouldn't do that, would he? After everything we had been through, would he do this to me?

"Hello, Shabnam," I answered, "Ray isn't here at the moment, but I'll get him to call you back."

"Thanks," she replied. I disconnected the call.

I did not really comprehend what happened next. By the time Ray-Jay returned, I was dressed again. I asked him why he had changed Shabnam's name in his phone and why he had told me that they were no longer in contact with each other. Every reply he gave me was a lie and I stormed out of the house telling him that I didn't want to be married to someone who couldn't be honest in his justification for his mishaps. I could no longer trust the only man I had ever trusted.

Within the next few hours, every memory of any time he may have been unfaithful or looked at another female lustfully, ran through my mind. I had to get revenge for this, I would make him believe in my love and then he would experience my wrath. But what if I forgave him before executing my plan? What was I doing even making plans? How could I say yes to someone for forever, knowing that I held this contemptible thought for them in the shadows of my mind?

The wedding was off, and the relationship was over!

Our friendship, however, did continue for a good few years more, that is until the extent of Ray-Jay's true colours was revealed to me, but that's another story.

Our Song: 'So Simple' ~ Alicia Keys.

My Song: 'Good Mourning' ~ India Arie.

Soiled
Chapter Three

～

"So, who did you tell?" Asked Eric.

I thought about the question.

I had told someone. I had told two people. I thought long and hard about the answer, and then it struck me like a jolt of electricity through my internal organs. My eyes felt like they were glitching, then that short sharp pain shot through my nasal bridge and water fell from my lower eyelids. Had I convinced myself for years that I had done enough, when the disturbing truth was that I had not done much at all?

The two I had told nine days after it happened, were who I had then felt to be my only true acquaintances. I met them at my new high school, and they had befriended me on the first day, initiating me into their crew as the new girl from Gunchester. One of them was and is to this day, a very dear, trustworthy and loyal friend. She listened to my story and took my word as truth without any need of evidence to support it. She comforted me and gave support through what I had then believed to be my most emotionally tortured episode in that series of my life.

The other, if an animal and not a human, would probably be an Ostrich. She refused to believe my version of events after she confronted the group leader and he insisted that – in her words,

"Why would he want to do that to me... (when I looked the way I did, short, black and overweight, although my mum and her friends called it puppy fat), ...when he could have her?"

I will never forget those words. As if pussy availability ever stopped a rapist. Could she actually hear what she was saying?

She was your averaged mixed heritage girl, slim build and as vain as anything you know to be that. She generally dressed like the younger sister in the movie, 'Coming to America,' was obsessed with name brands by designers who had at the time publicly disclosed that they would puke internally if they saw people of colour in their wares, and had medium texture thick, long hair.

She was much more attractive than me, especially for a male of his mental capacity. I agreed that there wasn't any reason for him doing it, but that did not stop him from assaulting me. She metaphorically put her hands over her ears, stuck her head in the sand and perched her ass out high for him to come get whenever he wanted or was bored enough to look her way.

After she had approached him, he must have gotten either scared or brave because he did exactly what he had threatened me, he would do if I told anyone.

He had warned me that if I told anyone they would just lie and say that I had let them 'run battery' on me. I had no clue of what that meant, as that wasn't slang where I came from and if it was, my ears had not been subjected to that kind of speech, but I knew what had happened and that he must have known it was wrong for him to feel the need to threaten me.

That was the beginning of my tortured early teenage years.

I only spoke the full extent of what had happened that day and the time surrounding it, to Teddy. After telling him, his reaction was to hunt each one of them down. I had begged him not to as I didn't want him getting involved in that way.

Over a year had passed, and so long as they kept their distance with me, all my vengeance would be left to Karma.

My Song: 'Feel No Way' ~ Janet Kay.

Best before 04/92
Chapter 3a

We walked in through the back door. It felt as if time had slowed down as everything seemed to be in slow motion.

As soon as his mother saw him, she began her torrent of accusations. Her face frowned, with each facial muscle moving individually. The left side of her lip twitched before opening to reveal her tongue flicking up and down with word pronunciation and her nostrils widened as the sound released.

I felt a shudder go through my body and I ran straight up the stairs into the bathroom. I stripped quickly and began my brutal body cleaning, I had the routine all worked out, I could not stop until I had removed at least two layers of skin. I couldn't bear to imagine that their handprints were still on me. Having watched many crime dramas, I knew that it took powerful cleaning products to remove fingerprints and secretions from certain surfaces.

I scrubbed intensely, my lady hole was bleeding, and the vigour I had used while scraping at the uneven tissue inside it could not have helped. I reached as far as I could inside myself trying to remove any trace of anything that felt like fluid. I couldn't even feel that I was inducing extra pain down there.

I did in the days following, but in that moment, every nerve ending in my body was numb.

I turned the radio up to drown out the sound of constant cussing coming from downstairs.

"I could drown me out," I whispered to myself as I looked around the bathroom.

It was steamy and my eyes were heavy and swollen from crying. I sighted the extension lead to which the radio was plugged and considered dropping the radio in with me as I noted two teardrops that had fallen around the volume dial. Then I gazed again at the walls, thinking about whether I really wanted to leave this world, this bathroom being the last room I saw.

I thought about the last conversation I had had with my mother, the last time I had seen my sisters, the last time I had played with my nephews and niece and I thought about my friends. I missed them all so desperately. None of this would have happened if I were home, but home was no longer home. I now resided in hell.

I should call my dad, I thought.

But how would I get hold of him, he had left the last residence I knew him to be at and the only other way would be via his friends.

Too long, maybe I should tell my brother, but that would start an all-out war. My brother would tell my other brothers that my dad would undoubtedly find out and just like that, total chaos would ensue.

It wasn't hot enough and this soap was no good. I remembered the warning I was given and instantly felt sick. The bile moved upwards; a metallic tasting watery substance began to flood into my mouth. Fluid beads rushed through my facial pores, bursting to the surface in what could only be described as a torrent of sweat.

My head hurt so bad, there was a banging behind my eyes, my legs were shaking profusely, my heart was beating so fast that my lungs were in pain. My whole body went weak as the water rose.

I heard a muffled banging on the door and emerged from underneath the water.

"Girl, how long do you need to be in there, come out now!"

My mother had arrived home and she was angry. Her friend had told her that I had used the last of the hot water from the boiler. This annoyed my mum because we were only staying at her friend's house while our boiler was being fixed and this was a disrespect of generosity. It would take up to two hours for the boiler to refill with hot water.

She didn't even ask how my day had gone. Her friend had answered every question she had asked her son by herself in her rant. He had taken the cursing trying to defend himself several times. Still, he was spoken over, to the point of his creating an unbroken silence on the happenings.

I was 12 and he was 11. How we were not noticed?

From that day onwards, my relationship with my mother was strained. She thought and told people that I was being rebellious and rude, I thought I was being assertive and independent.

Life was beginning to show me that only I could be responsible for me.

William and I did not discuss the events of that day until over two decades later. The silence had created a distance between us. In my late thirties, I called him to apologise for the detachment. He told me how relieved he was that we could finally do this and apologised to me for not saying anything. He apologised for anything and everything he did that may have harmed or injured me or my pride. I told him that we were too young to have had to deal with that alone.

Because we couldn't be heard that day, the words became harder to say with every day that followed. By the time the lie had been told, it was just too late.

People were talking, saying all sorts of horrible things and my mind was in a state. I hadn't even told my mother. What if the gossip reached her ears? I thought about how things would go if I told my mum. She would make sure that I went to the police. All of my family would know. This community we had moved into would be in total upheaval. The boys were well known and so were their families. What would I gain from it? I would have to speak in court and relive this ordeal over again, with each witness brought to the stand and each statement given. If justice was served, the boys would go to prison and

I would have handed them to a system designed to hold them down. But they didn't care about being held down, or they wouldn't have done this. I cared, though. They being locked up wouldn't give me back what they had taken from me. It wouldn't repair my body nor my mind. I had already seen the response of someone who was supposed to be my friend, I didn't want to see the reactions of people who felt they were given a reason to treat me like that.

The fact is that even though I went unnoticed by both of our mothers at that time, I was taught to consider others. I would never have dreamt of that being a possible happening, let alone being on the other side of that. Oh, the stuttered syllable beatings I would get from several members of my family.

Those boys knew what they were doing was wrong and they still went ahead. What had they been taught? What would their parents think today if I revealed their names? Would they even be shocked, or deep down do they know that their sons' harbour monsters inside them? Would they pick up on the fact that they had not instilled respect into the morals of their sons and that they had prepared men who would sacrifice innocence for ego? Did it even matter to them?

My disgust was with their mothers, but my vengeance was with them.

My song for them: 'Think' ~ Aretha Franklin.

Dear Karma
Chapter 3b

The school bell rang. I stayed stuck to my seat as the class rustled to get out of the room. Finishing the last verse of the song I was writing, I looked up to see Sarah reading from over my shoulder.

"I know that song," she said with excitement. "Love Takes Time, oh it's a good one. It's by Mariah Carey, isn't it? I didn't know you listened to Mariah, she is great, isn't she? The way she hits those high notes with such ease, an amazing voice she's got, don't you agree? Oh, I cannot believe you have the same taste in music as me, can you? This is one of those one in a million moments. How often do you sing a song in your head and then see someone writing the words to that same song? I never would have guessed. I'm going to have to read my horoscopes later and see if this was predicted. This is crazy, isn't it? Do you believe in horoscopes? I do, this is so unexpected. Mariah Carey is just magical, don't you think?"

She barely gave herself chance to take a breath, let alone allow, for me to reply to any of the quickfire questions she released in all her glee.

"Yes, it is, she does have a lovely voice, her content got me," I replied slowly, gathering my books together and getting up out of my seat.

"Are you heading for the No. 23?" She ranted on excitedly, "I've seen you at the bus stop, I'll walk with you if you're on your own, that's if you don't mind, we can talk Mariah on the way there. I knew there was something I liked about you. What are your favourites from the album? Mine are 'Emotions', 'Vision of Love', 'Can't Let Go', 'Someday', oh and track 11 of course. I practise all the time, but it's hard hitting them highs, and mi Mum complains that I'm frightening the cat."

We laughed and smiled with each other. I was on my own. I had deliberately waited until the first busload of pupils were at least eight minutes ahead of me in reaching the school gates.

The questions, assumptions and misinformed statements were just too much for me to contend with this week. I wanted Sarah's company too, it was a refreshing change from the usual boring boy, betrayals and botheration talks that normally pursued with the group I travelled with on my up days.

Today was a down day. I was stressed, feeling extremely lonely and missing my former home. I felt like a peacock in a kennel. I didn't belong here and very few people had even bothered to notice how depressed I had become.

Just a few weeks before I had made an attempt at suicide. I was so sad and feeling alienated. I didn't know who I could trust, and those I thought cared so much about me in my old hometown, had shown me otherwise. They had taken my mother's account of events as gospel without even speaking to me. I was lectured on obeying my mother and focusing more on my education, but no one ever focused on me, on the things I wasn't saying. What did they know about my life anyway? It was out of sight, out of mind. Everyone was getting on with their lives. Without mine, the only hindrance for them would be finding a babysitter for my little sister.

Music and Mariah were the topics of discussion all the way to the bus stop by the roundabout, two stops between both our houses. Sarah had promised to bring in her new Mariah Album as soon as it arrived from America. Her uncle had promised to get her a copy of *Music Box* for her 13th birthday, a month before it was released in the United Kingdom. We had discovered that we both had cassettes of her first two albums and agreed to bring our Walkman's to school for a singalong on the way home the next day.

I walked home, swinging my arms and singing, happier than I had been in a really long time. The clouds had cleared, and the sun was beaming through the treetops that lined the road towards my house. A bird flew by dropping a small white feather as it passed. I couldn't remember whether that was a good or a bad omen, but I thought it looked pretty and so I made a wish...

Dear Karma,

I know you see; I know nothing gets passed you and I really need you to do your thing. I have never hurt anybody intentionally (apart from that girl who called me a gollywog). I have tried to be a good daughter nearly all the time, but my mother does not understand me. I have tried to be a good friend to everyone I call a friend and even some that I don't. I have tried my best to stay out of trouble and not get involved in mix-up or unnecessary contention. I'm hurting so bad and I can't cope with the sight of those heartless beings. I have nothing to focus on but this, and so to avoid becoming bitter, I need you. I need you so bad it's twisting me up inside. If I take vengeance myself, there will be no turning back, and I won't even care about you or what you can do. So please Karma, while I still see you as an ally, work your magic in the worst way.

Your girl, N.

I repeated this to the moon, I repeated it to the stars. I repeated this for a whole week and then I handed it over to the bitch.

Though I was adamant then that Karma had to take vengeance for me. I felt that the energy I had placed into the universe to empower Karma was over extensive for some. I watched how life had treated them from a distance. I never went out of my way to find out anything, for some reason information always came to me coincidentally.

One year later I had re-visited for a Caribbean carnival. I had taken my daughter, who was two or three years old at the time. The streets are usually bustling with vibrantly clothed attendees making their way to the numerous street parties that are kept. I was heading to meet my sister at my DJ friend's house.

As I turned the corner, I bumped into one of the DJ's from that life-altering day. He was with his son, who was around the same age as my daughter. It had been years since I had seen him and although we had talked several times since the incident, this time was different.

His spirit told my spirit that it was time to talk the tings. He asked me if I was willing to accept his apology and forgive him for his involvement of that day. I was in total shock. None of them had ever spoken to me about it since the lead twat had shouted out that he had warned me what would happen if I opened my big mouth, from the top of an escalator in a shopping mall. I told him he was forgiven and thanked him for acknowledging the truth.

These lies had been going around about me for so long that I, myself, was beginning to wonder if I had indeed let them do that to me. It was like a breath of fresh air receiving his apology, but his life was taken in less than a year later while he was trying to defend his brother. I cried for him, I cried for his soul and I cried for his mother.

He had died as an honourable man in my eyes, for he had the strength and courage to admit his mistakes and repent for the effects his actions had had on the lives of others. Maybe becoming a parent had shown him the error of his ways but whatever it was, I was most appreciative of his admission and so sad that he was not able to be the father he intended to his son.

My song: 'Hero'~ Mariah Carey.

The Station
Chapter 3c

―――――――――― ∿ ――――――――――

Having not long moved to a new home, my mum was trying to find some sort of activity to help me settle in a new town. Back in our hometown, I had extracurricular activities nearly every day of the week. I had Choir practice, Orchestra practice, Woodwind practice, Girl Guides, Steel band, Basketball and Netball practice.

Here in Yorkshire, I had Trampoline practice one day a week, because there was no choir and there was no orchestra. Basketball and netball were replaced with hockey and trampolining. I wasn't much interested in hockey, it seemed like a toff's game to me. May as well have been in croquet or bowls.

I was class prefect at my old school, and I was the Stuart House team captain for my year also. We had four houses, Tudor, Hanover, Windsor and Stuart represented by a team captain and a deputy captain for each year group. The whole school was divided into four houses. Each pupil was given the opportunity to earn points for their house through academic, behavioural, extra-curricular or influential achievements. House points would be recorded and announced at the end of week assembly. At the end of the school year, the winning house would receive merits and bookshop vouchers as well as the school trophy and a celebratory meal.

Each form had a Prefect and Deputy Prefect, the leading example for the pupils in that year group and the year groups below. The Prefect and Deputy Prefect changed each term allowing for ample competition. They were responsible for giving out the end of term accreditations and HMV vouchers for term achievements.

Top marks in my form usually belonged to either myself or a girl named Ruth Lister. Ruth was my inspirer and rival. She encouraged me to do my best as it was like an unspoken competition between us. Both our names were always at the top of the achievement table, switching places, dancing together but always at the top. I had been a Deputy twice, once to Ruth and just before my mum changed town, Ruth had been mine. I can't remember if we ever spoke of our appreciation for each other, but if she ever reads this, she'll know I respected and admired her.

My new school had nothing to motivate me; no school competitions, no regional competitions, no school trips abroad, no achievement incentives, no membership bodies and no attainment awards. I thought that it was basically another primary school for older children.

Maybe I gave off a preparatory school privileged attitude to those that met me within the first few months of me being there. I honestly felt let down by what this curriculum was offering. It was only 50 miles up the motorway from our old town, so I couldn't comprehend how it could be so different. I was on my third year of German, they were on the second year. I was on my first year of Spanish, they were on the second year. Mathematics was taught with modules in a different order, things I did not know, had already been taught and what was being taught, I already knew. English was probably the closest to being on par with my previous curriculum. Music wasn't really a focus in this school's budget, and neither was sport. Thinking back, it's hard to know what this school actually specialised in. By the time I was in year ten, I had lost all interest in being the best that I could be academically. What was the point?

My mother had tried to find things to occupy my time. The community centre was filled with teenagers and young adults who were smoking, hustling or just looking for a place to be. I didn't like it there. The local library had a minimal selection of titles and the librarian always referred me to the main City Centre library. I couldn't get to the City Centre often because my school was in the opposite direction and I had to babysit my little sister, while my mum went to work most days.

Mum knew a few people who played music on the local pirate radio stations. One of them had informed her of an empty slot on a Saturday, so it was suggested that me and her friend's son, William, share the slot as a team. William and I were more like cousins because of the closeness of our mothers. In our culture, you tend to gain cousins through respect for the elders. If your mum had a friend, you would refer to her as aunty, because the roll they took on as a friend was much like that of an aunty. We thought the idea of becoming DJs was epic and immediately agreed. Both of us loved music and it was awesome when we started.

Before long, other DJs asked us to cover their show's when they were unable to attend. We had a wide audience of all ages and began getting a little popularity quite quickly.

One day after our show, we were asked to join the other young local DJ's at another station. We agreed as this was like networking. We were being invited into young popular circles. Although I felt nervous, William knew these boys well, so I went along to the next block of houses.

It was a three-floored house divided into flats. The first and second floor belonged to the radio station. It was much bigger than the station we were with. That was on the ground floor with two rooms, a kitchen and a toilet. We walked right up to the second floor where the broadcasting equipment was.

I glanced around before taking a seat next to William. The room was mostly empty. It was furnished with a couple of settees, a spinning back-support office chair with a rectangular table that the turntables, mixer and mic were placed on. The mic was nicer than the one our station had. The equipment was of a higher quality also. The window was in the sloped ceiling, so the light shone brightly through it. The walls were the shade of smoky magnolia and flyers covered a section of the wall, just above eye level for the seated DJ to announce during commercial breaks.

All the events were up-to-date, and a colour code differentiated the advertising package for each event. The Radio schedule for all the DJs was also on the wall with colour-coded music genres for each DJ. The studio was well taken care of and looked much more modern than the one I had become used to.

Our station had large windows covered with orange- and brown-patterned curtains. You would call them retro nowadays. They darkened the room and gave the studio a seventies rustic feel about it. There wasn't much unoccupied space compared to this one. I averted my eyes as I thought that I shouldn't be comparing the two, we had all we required at our studio. It was the first place to offer us an entrance into the entertainment industry. Even though this one was nicer, I did not feel as relaxed as I would have expected.

I began to watch the DJ's. They had an excellent rhythm between them. The energy was visible, and it was edifying to watch. They played the same music genres as we did, but they played the newest and most popular tracks.

I felt a little uneasy when I heard footsteps climbing the stairs. It sounded like more than two people and I began to get uncomfortable.

I pointed at my watch as I caught William's attention, it was time to go. A few more young boys had entered the room and I just felt ill at ease being the only female in there.

I told William that I was going to the toilet and that I would be ready once I had relieved myself.

I crouched over the toilet to urinate, looking down to make sure I was aiming through the hole. I could hear the stairs creaking and the sound of whispers and shuffling. I quickly wiped, pulled up my panties, fixed the drop on my skirt and flushed. The handwash basin was in the bathroom next door to the lavatory, I had spied it on entry.

As I opened the door to exit the slimline room, I felt it force back onto me and a charge of boys hurled me back with their body weight. I hit the floor, banging my head on the toilet bowl, and I felt a mass of weight fall on top of me. I was shouting and kicking, trying to punch or scratch anything I could. It was pointless. I could hear a commotion on the staircase and William's high-pitched half-broken voice. Hands were grabbing my sleeves and tugging at my breasts, knees were digging into my arms and fingers were on my legs. I screamed a dry throat scream. I bit at anything that came near my mouth. I heard material ripping. I wanted the floor to give way. I needed someone to come and save me. Why were they doing this to me?

The walk home was the longest and most silent. As we stepped in unison side by side, I looked over at William. He was bruised with broken skin around his swelling eye. His clothes were ripped like mine were, but he hadn't been raped.

My life was nothing now, I had nothing now. The one thing that was mine that no-one could see was gone. I was soiled, ruined, spoiled. My virginity had been stolen and I was absolutely devastated. I was in a strange town with horrible people and I just wanted my mum, but she was at work as per usual. I wanted my sisters, I wanted my old house, I wanted my old bedroom. I wanted the me that I had looked at in the mirror before I left the house this morning, but she was nowhere to be seen, she was gone, she was no more, she had left and could not return. That girl had a premature death and would not be seen ever again.

I needed a bath so, so badly. I felt dirty, my skin was crawling, and I wanted bleach, Dettol, jiff, bay rum and hot water.

My song: 'Stole' ~ Kelly Rowland.

About The Author

British born of Caribbean parents, the author is a four-decade strong, analytically minded female. Beginning her career in the Hospitality and Health industries, then continuing into Communications Law and Business. Having a strong desire to help and empower others since young, she has  committed professions which allow for this. Self-investing in continuous education and holding the belief that learning is ongoing till the day of our last breaths. She holds faith as her staff and views each day as a new adventure.

The author would like to share some of the experiences she has had, in the hope that it reaches the hearts and minds of those who read it. Giving insight wherever necessary and comfort wherever needed.

Releasing through the charity Finding Nyah, which aims to empower the future generations by way of community communication and enhancement. The author believes that her journey will prevent hindrances in the understanding of mental health issues that stop communities from developing and progressing.

www.marciampublishing.com

Printed in Great Britain
by Amazon